讓世界認識台灣

經濟的繁榮、政治的民主，已經讓世界聽到台灣的聲音。我們每天在台灣品嚐的、感受的、經歷的、閱讀的、記憶的、欣賞的事物，要如何和老外分享？讓他們知道這塊土地的過去與現在，美麗與哀愁。

世界越來越小，朋友越來越多。當老外問你："Where are you from?" 你準備如何回答？只是 Taiwan，還是……

這本書搜集了 70 個老外詢問度最高的問題，每個問題整理出三個重點，讓你可以一針見血地回答。你也可以經由「背景說明」的部分：(1)認識每個句子不同的呈現方式；(2)從中學得一些同義字；(3)了解更多美國人的口語用法；或(4)知道更多的相關資訊。

這不是一本台灣旅遊手冊，應該算是「國民外交手冊」，它給你台灣的全貌，整理出每一個主題的重點。你可以不用全部背起來，但其中的關鍵字最好能塞進腦袋，以便運用。

你正準備出國嗎？你的外國朋友將飛來台灣嗎？這本書已經為你準備好所有問題的答案。

編者 謹識

Taiwan is a place unlike any other!

Taiwan has survived, persevered and prospered. Its history is colorful and proud. Its people are spirited and determined. This island is truly one of the world's most dynamic.

This book was written to give you a brief insight into this fascinating, complex and fast-changing society. It's also a learning source for non-English speakers. Enjoy this book and learn from it. It's both informative and educational.

Practice asking and answering these questions. They are so common and useful that you could ask them about any country, anywhere. (You only have to replace the names.)

Visitors to Taiwan won't be disappointed! It's an amazing mixture of East and West. Here traditional Chinese culture is combined with modern Western commercialism. The cities are bustling with activity. The island has beautiful mountain forests and national parks. Taiwan is never boring. There is something here to satisfy everyone. You name it, Taiwan has it!

台灣是個獨一無二的地方！

台灣從困境中倖存，努力不懈，終至繁榮興盛。它的歷史多彩而值得驕傲，它的人民生氣勃勃而信念堅定，它真的是世界上最有活力的一座島嶼。

這本書的撰寫，是希望提供給你這迷人的、多樣的、快速轉變的社會一個簡要的觀察，而且對不是以英語為母語的人來說，是個學習的資源。善用這本書，並且從中學習吧。它兼具了知識性與教育性。

要練習問和答這些問題，它們很普遍而且實用，你可以在任何國家問這些問題。(只要把名稱換掉就可以了。)

來台灣觀光不會讓你失望！它是一個驚人的東西方綜合體。這裡結合了傳統的中國文化與現代的西方商業主義，市況熙攘而忙碌。這座島嶼有美麗的山林和國家公園，台灣絕對不會讓你覺得無聊，它能滿足每個人的需求。你說得出來的，台灣都有！

CONTENTS

Chapter 2 風俗 Customs

Chapter 3 文化 Culture

Chapter 4 節日 *Festivals*

Chapter 5　景點 *Tour Sites*

本書製作過程

　　本書能夠順利完成，是靠一整個團隊的力量。經美籍老師 Andy Swarzman、Edward C. Yulo、Tony Chen 及謝靜芳老師等細心校訂，Laura E. Stewart 總校閱，白雪嬌小姐負責設計專業的封面，黃淑貞小姐負責版面設計，以及蔡資敏小姐提供部份圖片，非常感謝他們辛苦的付出。

Taiwan Map

馬祖
Matsu

金門縣
Kinmen County

陽明山國家公園
Yangmingshan National Park

台北市 Taipei City

基隆市
Keelung City

桃園縣
Taoyuan County

台北縣
Taipei County

新竹市
Hsinchu City

新竹縣
Hsinchu County

宜蘭縣
Ilan County

苗栗縣
Miaoli County

台中市
Taichung City

台中縣 Taichung County

台灣海峽
Taiwan Strait

日月潭
Sun Moon Lake

太魯閣峽谷
Taroko Gorge

彰化縣
Changhwa County

花蓮縣
Hualien County

雲林縣
Yunlin County

南投縣
Nantou County

嘉義縣
Chia-I County

阿里山
Alishan

太平洋
Pacific Ocean

嘉義市
Chia-I City

澎湖縣
Penghu County

台南縣
Tainan County

高雄縣
Kaohsiung County

台東縣
Taitung County

台南市
Tainan City

綠島
Green Island

高雄市
Kaohsiung City

屏東縣
Pingtung County

墾丁國家公園
Kenting National Park

蘭嶼
Orchid Island

巴士海峽 Luzon Strait

我應該如何稱呼台灣？

What should I call Taiwan?

Now Taiwan's official name is the Republic of China.

Taiwan was once called Formosa.

Most people just call Taiwan "Taiwan."

**

official〔ə'fɪʃəl〕adj. 官方的；正式的
republic〔rɪ'pʌblɪk〕n. 共和國
the Republic of China 中華民國
once〔wʌns〕adv. 曾經
Formosa〔fɔr'mosə〕n. 福爾摩莎

【背景說明】

1. *What should I call Taiwan?*

這句話的意思是「我應該如何稱呼台灣？」也可說成：What's the most widely accepted name for Taiwan?（台灣最被接受的名稱是什麼？）或 What's the most common name for Taiwan?（台灣最常見的名稱是什麼？）。

這是外國人常問的問題，他們或許也會問：

Is Taiwan a country?（台灣是不是一個國家？）
Is it separate from the mainland?
（它是不是和大陸分開？）

Is it independent?（台灣是不是獨立了？）
What does R.O.C. mean?（R.O.C. 是什麼意思？）
What does R.O.C. stand for?（R.O.C. 是代表什麼？）

【accepted〔ək'sɛptɪd〕*adj.* 公認的　*stand for* 代表】

2. *Taiwan's official name is the Republic of China.*

official〔ə'fɪʃəl〕*adj.* 官方的；正式的
republic〔rɪ'pʌblɪk〕*n.* 共和國
the Republic of China 中華民國

這句話的意思是「台灣的正式名稱是『中華民國』。」

official 的主要意思是「官方的」，在此作「正式的」解，等於 formal。上面句子中的 official，可用 formal 取代。

通常國名之前不加定冠詞 the，但如果國名中含有普通名詞，則必須加 the，如：the Republic of China（中華民國）、the United States of America（美國）、the United Arab Emirates（阿拉伯聯合大公國）。

3. *Taiwan was once called Formosa.*

once〔wʌns〕*adv.* 曾經
Formosa〔fɔr'mosə〕*n.* 福爾摩莎

這句話的意思是「台灣曾經被稱作福爾摩莎。」也可說成：

Taiwan used to be called Formosa.
（台灣從前被稱作「福爾摩莎」。）
Taiwan originally was called Formosa.
（台灣最初被稱作「福爾摩莎」。）
Taiwan's earliest western name was Formosa.
（台灣最早的西方名稱是「福爾摩莎」。）

used to 以前　originally〔ə'rɪdʒənḷɪ〕*adv.* 最初；原本
western〔'wɛstən〕*adj.* 西方的

4. *Most people just call Taiwan "Taiwan."*

這句話的意思是「大部分的人只是稱呼台灣『台灣』。」也可說成：

Now, everybody just simply calls Taiwan "Taiwan."（現在，每個人只是稱呼台灣『台灣』。）
【simply〔'sɪmplɪ〕*adv.* 只是】

Question 2

台灣有多大？

How big is Taiwan?

It's about the same size as Holland.

It's about 394 km long and 144 km wide.

Its total area is about 36,000 square kilometers.

** ──────────────────────

Holland ('hɑlənd) *n.* 荷蘭　　**km** 公里 (= *kilometer*)
wide (waɪd) *adj.* 寬…的　　total ('totļ) *adj.* 全部的
area ('ɛrɪə) *n.* 面積　　square (skwɛr) *adj.* 平方的
kilometer ('kɪlə,mitɚ) *n.* 公里

【背景說明】

1. ***How big is Taiwan?***

　　　這句話的意思是「台灣有多大？」也可說成：

　　About how big is Taiwan? (台灣大約多大？)

　　What is the size of Taiwan?

　　(台灣有多大？)

　　How large is Taiwan? (台灣多大？)

　　What is Taiwan like in terms of size?

　　(以大小的角度來說，台灣怎麼樣？)

　　【*in terms of* 以…的角度；從…觀點】

2. ***It is about the same size as Holland.***

size〔saɪz〕*n.* 大小；尺寸

Holland〔'hɑlənd〕*n.* 荷蘭

　　　這句話的意思是「它的大小和荷蘭差不多。」

也可說成：

　　It's about as big as Holland.

　　(它和荷蘭差不多一樣大。)

　　Taiwan and Holland are about the same size.

　　(台灣和荷蘭差不多一樣大小。)

　　Taiwan is equal to Holland in size.

　　(台灣的大小和荷蘭相同。)

　　【equal〔'ikwəl〕*adj.* 同樣的；相等的】

Holland 是「荷蘭」的俗稱，其正式的國名是 the Netherlands；而「荷蘭人」的複數形是 the Dutch，單數是 Dutchman（單數）。口語中常用的 Go Dutch. 意思就是「各付各的。」其中的 Dutch 是形容詞，表「荷蘭人作風的」。【Netherlands (ˈnɛðələndz) n. 荷蘭 Dutch (dʌtʃ) n. 荷蘭語；荷蘭人　adj. 荷蘭（人、語）的】

3. **It's about 394 km long and 144 km wide.**

km 公里 (= *kilometer*)　　wide (waɪd) adj. 寬…的

這句話的意思是「它大約 394 公里長，144 公里寬。」也可說成：

It's 394 km in length and 144 km in width.
（它的長度是 394 公里，寬度是 144 公里。）
It has a length of 394 km and a width of 144 km.
（它的長度是 394 公里，寬度是 144 公里。）
【length (lɛŋθ) n. 長度　　width (wɪdθ) n. 寬度】

美國人習慣以英哩來計算長度的單位，1 公里約等於 0.6215 英哩，所以台灣的長度大約是 244 英哩，寬 89 英哩。

4. **Its total area is about 36,000 square kilometers.**

total (ˈtotḷ) adj. 全部的　　area (ˈɛrɪə) n. 面積
square (skwɛr) adj. 平方的
kilometer (ˈkɪlə,mitə) n. 公里

這句話的意思是「它的總面積大約是三萬六千平方公里。」也可說成：It's about 36,000 sq. km. (它大約是三萬六千平方公里。)【sq. 平方的 (= square)】

台灣在哪裡？

Where is Taiwan?

Taiwan sits on the east edge of the Asian continent.

It's located about 160 km off the southeastern coast of China.

It lies among a chain of islands from Japan to the Philippines.

**

sit〔sɪt〕v. 位於　east〔ist〕adj. 東方的　edge〔ɛdʒ〕n. 邊緣
Asian〔'eʃən〕adj. 亞洲的　continent〔'kɑntənənt〕n. 大陸
locate〔lo'ket〕v. 使位於　off〔ɔf〕adv. 在…之外
southeastern〔,sauθ'istən〕adj. 東南的　coast〔kost〕n. 海岸
lie〔laɪ〕v. 位於　chain〔tʃen〕n. 一連串
Philippines〔'fɪlə,pinz〕n. pl. 菲律賓群島

【背景說明】

1. *Where is Taiwan?*

這句話的意思是「台灣在哪裡？」也可說成：

Where is Taiwan located? (台灣位於哪裡？)
Where is Taiwan's location? (台灣的位置在哪裡？)
Where is Taiwan on the map?
(台灣在地圖上的哪裡？)

【location (loˋkeʃən) *n.* 位置；地點   map (mæp) *n.* 地圖】

2. *Taiwan sits on the east edge of the Asian continent.*

sit (sɪt) *v.* 位於   east (ist) *adj.* 東方的
edge (ɛdʒ) *n.* 邊緣   Asian (ˋeʃən) *adj.* 亞洲的
continent (ˋkɑntənənt) *n.* 大陸

這句話的意思是「台灣位於亞洲大陸東方的邊緣。」
也可說成：

Taiwan is located east of the Asian continent.
(台灣位於亞洲大陸的東方。)
Taiwan is east of the Asian continent.
(台灣位於亞洲大陸的東方。)
Taiwan is east of continental Asia.
(台灣位於亞洲大陸的東方。)

be east of~   在~的東方
continental (ˌkɑntəˋnɛntḷ) *adj.* 大陸的

sit 通常指「坐」，但也可以表國家或建築物等「坐落」於某處。下面兩個句子中的 be located 及 lie 也可用以表國家及建築物坐落於某處。

3. *It's located about 160 km off the southeastern coast of China.*

locate〔loˈket〕v. 使位於　*be located*　位於
off〔ɔf〕adv. 在…之外
southeastern〔ˌsauθˈistɚn〕adj. 東南的
coast〔kost〕n. 海岸

　　這句話的意思是「它位於中國東南岸約一百六十公里外。」

　　當 locate 用來表示建築物或國家所在的位置時，通常須用被動語態 be located「位於～」。

4. *It lies among a chain of islands from Japan to the Philippines.*

among〔əˈmʌŋ〕prep. 在…當中
chain〔tʃən〕n. 一連串　island〔ˈaɪlənd〕n. 島
Philippines〔ˈfɪləˌpinz〕n. pl. 菲律賓群島

　　這句話的意思是「它位於日本到菲律賓群島的列島之間。」

　　lie 的基本意思是作「躺」解，在此作「位於」解，須用主動語態。

　　chain 通常指「項鍊、鍊子」，在此表「一連串」，而 a chain of～，則是指「一連串的～」。

　　國名通常都不加 the（請參考 Question 1 的背景説明），句中的 the Philippines 是指「菲律賓群島」，也可作「菲律賓共和國」解。

Question **4**　台灣的人口有多少？

What's the population of Taiwan?

There are about 23 million people in Taiwan.

Taiwan's population density is the second highest in the world.

Ninety percent of the population lives on the west coast.

**

population (ˌpɑpjəˈleʃən) *n.* 人口；居民

million (ˈmɪljən) *n.* 百萬　density (ˈdɛnsətɪ) *n.* 密度

percent (pəˈsɛnt) *n.* 百分比

west (wɛst) *adj.* 西方的　coast (kost) *n.* 海岸

【背景説明】

1. ***What's the population of Taiwan?***

   population (ˌpɑpjəˈleʃən) *n.* 人口

   這句話的意思是「台灣的人口有多少？」也可説成：

   What's Taiwan's population?

   （台灣的人口有多少？）

   How large is the population of Taiwan?

   （台灣的人口有多少？）

   How many people are there in Taiwan?

   （台灣有多少人？）

   population 是指「人口總數」，是一個數字，只能
   用 what（這個數字是什麼）或 how large（這個數字多
   大），不能用 how many（這個數字有幾個）來問。

2. ***There are about 23 million people in Taiwan.***

   million (ˈmɪljən) *n.* 百萬

   這句話的意思是「台灣大約有兩千三百萬人。」
   也可説成：

   Taiwan has close to 23 million people.

   （台灣有將近兩千三百萬人。）

   Taiwan's population is about 23 million.

   （台灣的人口大約有兩千三百萬人。）

   The population of Taiwan is about 23 million.

   （台灣的人口大約有兩千三百萬人。）【*close to* 將近】

3. *Taiwan's population density is the second highest in the world.*

density (ˈdɛnsətɪ) *n.* 密度
the second highest 第二高的

這句話的意思是「台灣的人口密度是全世界第二高。」
也可說成：

Taiwan is very densely populated.
（台灣的人口很稠密。）

Taiwan has the second highest population
density in the world.
（台灣有全世界第二高的人口密度。）

Taiwan is number two (#2) in the world
in population density.
（台灣的人口密度是全世界第二名。）

densely (ˈdɛnslɪ) *adv.* 稠密地
populate (ˈpɑpjəˌlet) *v.* 居住於

4. *Ninety percent of the population live in the west coast.*

percent (pəˈsɛnt) *n.* 百分比

west (wɛst) *adj.* 西方的   coast (kost) *n.* 海岸

這句話的意思是「百分之九十的人口住在西岸。」
也可說成：

Taiwan's west coast is home to ninety percent
of the population.
（百分之九十人口的家在台灣西岸。）

台灣主要的族群有哪些？

What are the main ethnic groups in Taiwan?

There are four major ethnic groups in Taiwan.

They are the aborigines, the Hakka, the Fujianese and the Mainlanders.

The Hakka and the Fujianese comprise about 85% of the population.

**

main〔men〕*adj.* 主要的　　ethnic〔'εθnɪk〕*adj.* 人種的
major〔'medʒɚ〕*adj.* 主要的
aborigine〔ˌæbə'rɪdʒəni〕*n.* 原住民
Hakka〔'hɑk'kɑ〕*n.* 客家人
Mainlander〔'menˌlændɚ〕*n.* 外省人
Fujianese〔fu'dʒɪəniz〕*n.* 福建人（在此指「閩南人」）
comprise〔kəm'praɪz〕*v.* 構成

【背景說明】

1. *What are the main ethnic groups in Taiwan?*

main〔men〕*adj.* 主要的　　ethnic〔'εθnɪk〕*adj.* 人種的

這句話的意思是「台灣主要的族群有哪些？」也可說成：

What major groups make up Taiwan's population?
（台灣的人口是由什麼主要的族群組成？）
What's the ethnic background of the Taiwanese?
（台灣人種的背景是什麼？）

make up 組成　　originally〔ə'rɪdʒənḷɪ〕*adv.* 最初；本來
background〔'bæk,graund〕*n.* 背景

2. *There are four major ethnic groups in Taiwan.*

major〔'medʒɚ〕*adj.* 主要的

這句話的意思是「台灣有四個主要族群。」也可說成：Taiwan has four main ethnic groups.（台灣有四個主要的族群。）

3. *They are the aborigines, the Hakka, the Fujianese and the Mainlanders.*

aborigine〔,æbə'rɪdʒəni〕*n.* 原住民
Hakka〔'hɑk'kɑ〕*n.* 客家人
Fujianese〔fu'dʒɪəniz〕*n.* 福建人
Mainlander〔'men,lændɚ〕*n.* 外省人

這句話的意思是「他們是原住民、客家人、福建人，及外省人。」也可說成：

The aborigines, the Hakka, the Fujianese
　　and the Mainlanders make up Taiwan.
（原住民、客家人、閩南人和外省人組成台灣。）

Taiwan's population consists of the aborigines,
　　the Hakka, the Fujianese and the Mainlanders.
（台灣的人口是由原住民、客家人、閩南人，和外省人組成。）
【*consist of* 由～組成】

　　　　mainland 是指對附近島嶼或半島來說，是主要的
一塊陸地，所以「中國大陸」被稱爲 the Mainland of
China，或 mainland China，而出生於 mainland 的
人就是 mainlander。

4. *The Hakka and the Fujianese comprise about 85%*
of the population.
comprise〔kəm'praɪz〕*v.* 構成

　　　　這句話的意思是「客家人和閩南人構成了約百分
之八十五的人口。」也就是「百分之八十五的人口是
客家人和福建人。」

　　　　comprise 這個動詞，有兩個用法：
①「整體」由「部分」構成、包含：
　　The United States comprises fifty states.
　　　（美國有五十個州。）
②「部分」構成「整體」【常用被動語態，介系詞用 of】
　　Water is comprised of oxygen and hydrogen.
　　　（水是用氫跟氧所組成。）

Question 6 誰是原住民？

Who are the aborigines?

They were Taiwan's earliest inhabitants.

They migrated here from Pacific islands thousands of years ago.

They are often called "the mountain people."

** ————————————————

aborigine〔͵æbə'rɪdʒəni〕 *n.* 原住民

inhabitant〔ɪn'hæbətənt〕 *n.* 居民

migrate〔'maɪgret〕 *v.* 移居

Pacific〔pə'sɪfɪk〕 *adj.* 太平洋的

【背景説明】

1. ***Who are the aborigines?***

   aborigine〔͵æbə'rɪdʒəni〕*n.* 原住民

   > 這句話的意思是「誰是原住民？」也可説成：
   >
   > Who are the indigenous people?
   >
   > （誰是原住民？）
   >
   > Tell me about the aborigine people.
   >
   > （告訴我關於原住民的事。）
   >
   > 【 indigenous〔ɪn'dɪdʒənəs〕*adj.* 原產的 】

2. ***They were Taiwan's earliest inhabitants.***

   inhabitant〔ɪn'hæbətənt〕*n.* 居民

   > 　　這句話的意思是「他們是台灣最早的居民。」也
   >
   > 可説成：
   >
   > They were the original settlers of Taiwan.
   >
   > （他們是台灣最早的移民。）
   >
   > Taiwan's first inhabitants were aborigines.
   >
   > （台灣最早的居民是原住民。）
   >
   > original〔ə'rɪdʒənl̩〕*adj.* 最早的；原始的
   >
   > settler〔'sɛtlɚ〕*n.* 移民
   >
   > 　　英文單字字尾 ant 表「人」，如 inhabit<u>ant</u>
   >
   > （居民）、serv<u>ant</u>（僕人）、gi<u>ant</u>（巨人）、mig<u>rant</u>
   >
   > （移民）。

3. ***They migrated here from Pacific islands
thousands of years ago.***

migrate (＇maɪgret) *v.* 移居
Pacific (pəˊsɪfɪk) *adj.* 太平洋的
thousands of 數千的

　　這句話的意思是「數千年前，原住民從太平洋群島
移居到這裡。」也可説成：

Historians say the aborigines arrived in Taiwan
　　about 14,000 years ago.
（歷史學家說，原住民大約在一萬四千年前來到台灣。）

Theory has it that the aborigines came from
　　Malay and Polynesian islands.
（理論指出，原住民是來自於馬來半島和玻里尼西
　　亞群島。）

historian (hɪsˊtorɪən) *n.* 歷史學家
theory (ˊθiərɪ) *n.* 理論　　***theory has it that*** 理論指出
Malay (məˊle) *adj.* 馬來半島的
Polynesian (ˌpɑləˊniʃən) *adj.* 玻里尼西亞的

4. ***They are often called "the mountain people."***

　　這句話的意思是「他們常被稱爲『山地人』。」也
可説成："Mountain people" is a common name
for aborigines. (『山地人』是原住民常見的稱呼。)

Question 7

誰是客家人？

Who are the Hakka?

The Hakka are a minority group.

They came from southern China hundreds of years ago.

The name Hakka means "guest" in Cantonese.

**

Hakka〔'hɑk'kɑ〕*n.* 客家人
minority〔mə'nɔrətɪ〕*n.* 少數
southern〔'sʌðən〕*adj.* 南方的；南部的
hundreds of 數百的　　guest〔gɛst〕*n.* 客人
Cantonese〔ˌkæntən'iz〕*n.* 廣東話

【背景說明】

1. ***Who are the Hakka?***

   Hakka (ˈhɑkˈkɑ) *n.* 客家人

   　　這句話的意思是「誰是客家人？」也可說成：

   Can you tell me about the Hakka people?

   （你可以告訴我關於客家人的事嗎？）

   What's the story on the Hakka people?

   （客家人的來歷是什麼？）

   　　story 一般是指「故事」，每個人都有自己的故
   事，所以它也可指人的「身世、來歷」。

2. ***The Hakka are a minority group.***

   minority (məˈnɔrətɪ) *n.* 少數

   　　這句話的意思是「客家人是少數民族。」也可說成：

   The Hakka population is small.

   （客家的人口數很小。）

   The percentage of Hakka in Taiwan is low.

   （客家人佔台灣人口比率的少數。）

   The Hakka comprise about 15% of the
   population. （客家人約佔了人口數的百分之十五。）

   【percentage (pəˈsɛntɪdʒ) *n.* 比率；部份】

   　　minority 的反義詞是 majority (məˈdʒɔrətɪ) *n.*
   多數。

3. ***They came from southern China hundreds of***
years ago.

southern（'sʌðən）*adj.* 南方的；南部的

這句話的意思是「數百年前他們來自中國南部。」
也可說成：

The Hakka arrived from southern China
centuries ago.

（客家人幾世紀前來自中國南部。）

The Hakka arrived from China centuries ago.

（客家人幾世紀前來自中國。）

4. ***The name Hakka means "guest" in Cantonese.***

guest（gɛst）*n.* 客人
Cantonese（͵kæntən'iz）*n.* 廣東話

這句話的意思是「客家這個名稱在廣東話是『客
人』的意思。」也可說成：

The name Hakka has the meaning of guest
in Cantonese.

（客家這個名稱在廣東話有客人的意思。）

The term Hakka, in Cantonese, means guest.

（客家這個名詞在廣東話中，意思是客人。）

【term（tɝm）*n.* 名詞；用語】

Question 8

誰是福建人？

Who are the Fujianese?

They are migrants from Fujian Province in China.

Fujianese comprise seventy percent of Taiwan's population.

The Fujianese language is almost the same as modern Taiwanese.

**

Fujianese (fuˋdʒɪəniz) *n.* 福建人（話）
migrant (ˋmaɪgrənt) *n.* 移居者
Fujian (fuˋdʒɪən) *n.* 福建   province (ˋpravɪns) *n.* 省
comprise (kəmˋpraɪz) *v.* 由⋯構成
modern (ˋmadən) *adj.* 現代的

【背景説明】

1. *Who are the Fujianese?*

這句話的意思是「誰是福建人？」也可以説：

Please give me some background on the
Fujianese.（請你告訴我一些福建人的背景。）

Please give me the history of the Fujianese.

（請你告訴我福建人的歷史。）

【give〔gɪv〕v. 告訴　background〔'bæk,graʊnd〕n. 背景】

2. *They are migrants from Fujian Province in China.*

migrant〔'maɪgrənt〕n. 移居者

Fujian〔fu'dʒɪən〕n. 福建　province〔'pravɪns〕n. 省

這句話的意思是「他們是來自中國福建省的移
民。」也可説成：

They migrated from China's Fujian Province.

（他們遷徙自中國福建省。）

They are people from Fujian who immigrated
to Taiwan.（他們是從福建移民來台灣的人。）

migrate 是指「移居」，移出或移入均可使用這
個字，immigrate 是指「（自國外）移入」，emigrate
是指「移出（前往他國）」。

migrate〔'maɪgret〕v. 移居　emigrate〔'ɛmə,gret〕v. 移出
immigrate〔'ɪmə,gret〕v. 移入

3. *Fujianese comprise 70% of Taiwan's population*.
comprise〔kəm'praɪz〕*v.* 構成

這句話的意思是「福建人構成百分之七十的台灣
人口。」也可說成：

Fujianese make up a large majority of Taiwan's
population. (福建人是台灣人口的大多數。)
Most current Taiwanese have a Fujian
background.
(現今大部分的台灣人都有福建的背景。)
The Fujian people make up about two-thirds
of Taiwan's population.
(福建人組成大約三分之二的台灣人口。)

majority〔mə'dʒɔrətɪ〕*n.* 大多數　current〔'kʒənt〕*adj.* 現今的
make up 組成　**two-thirds** 三分之二

4. *The Fujianese language is almost the same as modern
Taiwanese*.

這句話的意思是「福建話幾乎和現在的台灣話
一樣。」也可說成：

The Fujianese and Taiwanese are closely related.
(福建話和台灣話有很密切的關聯。)
Taiwanese is almost identical to Fujianese.
(台灣話幾乎和福建話一模一樣。)

closely〔'kloslɪ〕*adv.* 密切地　related〔rɪ'letɪd〕*adj.* 有關聯的
identical〔aɪ'dɛntɪkļ〕*adj.* 相同的

誰是外省人？

Who are the Mainlanders?

They are from many provinces of mainland China.

They retreated here after fighting the Communists.

Most were Nationalist officials, soldiers and their families.

**

Mainlander〔'men͵lændə〕 *n.* 外省人

province〔'prɑvɪns〕 *n.* 省　　***mainland China***　中國大陸

retreat〔rɪ'trit〕 *v.* 撤退　　fight〔faɪt〕 *v.* 與…作戰

Communist〔'kɑmju͵nɪst〕 *n.* 共產黨員

Nationalist〔'næʃənl̩ɪst〕 *adj.* 國家主義者的（在此指國民黨員的）

official〔ə'fɪʃəl〕 *n.* 官員　　soldier〔'soldʒə〕 *n.* 軍人

【背景說明】

1. **Who are the Mainlanders?**
   Mainlander〔'men,lændə〕 *n.* 外省人

   > 這句話的意思是「誰是外省人?」也可説成:

   What's the history of the Mainlanders?
   (外省人的來歷是什麼?)
   What does the term Mainlanders mean?
   (外省人這個詞是什麼意思?)

2. **They are from many provinces of mainland China.**
   province〔'pravɪns〕 *n.* 省   **mainland China** 中國大陸

   > 這句話的意思是「他們來自中國大陸的許多省
   > 分。」也可説成:

   Mainlanders, like their name, come from the
   mainland. (外省人,就像他們的名稱 —— 來自大陸。)
   A Mainlander is someone from China.
   (外省人就是來自中國大陸的人。)

3. **They retreated here after fighting the Communists.**
   retreat〔rɪ'trit〕 *v.* 撤退   fight〔faɪt〕 *v.* 與…作戰
   Communist〔'kamju,nɪst〕 *n.* 共產黨員

   > 這句話的意思是「他們與共產黨交戰失利之後撤
   > 退來這裡。」也可説成:

Mainlanders arrived here after an unsuccessful
war with the Communists.

（外省人在與共產黨的戰爭失敗之後來到這裡。）

Mainlanders came to Taiwan to regroup and
regain mainland China.

（外省人來到台灣，是爲了重新部署並收回中國大陸。）

retreat「撤退」本身含有受到敵人的壓力、戰爭失
利的意思，所以即使句中未提及輸贏，也能明白其意。

unsuccessful〔ˌʌnsəkˈsɛsfəl〕*adj.* 失敗的
regroup〔riˈgrup〕*v.* 再集成群　　regain〔rɪˈgen〕*v.* 收回

4. *Most were Nationalist officials, soldiers and their families.*

Nationalist〔ˈnæʃənlɪst〕*adj.* 國家主義者的(在此指國民黨員的)
official〔əˈfɪʃəl〕*n.* 官員　　soldier〔ˈsoldʒɚ〕*n.* 軍人

這句話的意思是「大部分是國民政府官員、軍人和
他們的家人。」也可説成：

Almost all the Mainlanders were government
or military officials and their families.

（幾乎所有的外省人，都是政府或軍隊的官員和他們的家人。）

Most Mainlanders were KMT soldiers, their
leaders and their families.

（大部分的外省人是國民黨的軍人、他們的領導人及他
們的家人。）

【KMT = Kuomintang〔ˈkwomɪnˌtæŋ〕*n.* 國民黨】

Question
10　台灣人是怎麼樣的人？

What are Taiwanese like?

Taiwanese are warm-hearted, hard
　working people.
They are also traditional and
　conservative.
Taiwanese are very loyal to their
　families.

** ————————————

warm-hearted (ˈwɔrmˈhɑrtɪd) adj. 熱心的
hard (hɑrd) adv. 努力地　working (ˈwɜkɪŋ) adj. 工作的
traditional (trəˈdɪʃənḷ) adj. 傳統的
conservative (kənˈsɜvətɪv) adj. 保守的
loyal (ˈlɔɪəl) adj. 忠誠的

【背景説明】

1. *What are Taiwanese like?*

這句話的意思是「台灣人是怎麼樣的人？」也可説成：

What's a typical person in Taiwan like?
（典型的台灣人是怎麼樣的？）
What are some common characteristics of
the Taiwanese?（台灣人有哪些普遍的特性？）

typical (ˈtɪpɪkl̩) *adj.* 典型的
characteristic (ˌkærɪktəˈrɪstɪk) *n.* 特性

What + be 動詞 + 人事物 + like? 是美國人常用的句型，只要是對任何「人事物」不清楚，而想詢問他人時，都可以使用這個句型。如：What are your classmates like?（你的同學人怎樣？）What's your new house like?（你的新房子是什麼樣子？）

2. *Taiwanese are warm-hearted, hard working people.*

warm-hearted (ˈwɔrmˈhɑrtɪd) *adj.* 熱心的
hard (hɑrd) *adv.* 努力地　　working (ˈwɜkɪŋ) *adj.* 工作的

這句話的意思是「台灣人是熱心且工作勤奮的民族。」也可説成：The Taiwanese are kind, diligent people. (台灣人是友善而且勤奮的民族。)

【diligent (ˈdɪlədʒənt) *adj.* 勤勉的】

hearted 表「有…心的」，通常以複合字的形態出現，如：kind-hearted (好心的)、broken-hearted (心碎的) 等。

3. ***They are also traditional and conservative.***
traditional (trə'dɪʃənḷ) *adj.* 傳統的
conservative (kən'sɜvətɪv) *adj.* 保守的

這句話的意思是「他們也很傳統和保守。」也可
說成：

They are respectful of "the old ways."
（他們尊重舊習。）
They respect traditional customs.
（他們尊重傳統的習俗。）

respectful (rɪ'spɛktfəl) *adj.* 尊敬的
respect (rɪ'spɛkt) *v.* 尊敬；尊重

4. ***Taiwanese are very loyal to their families.***
loyal ('lɔɪəl) *adj.* 忠誠的

這句話的意思是「台灣人非常忠於他們的家庭。」
也可說成：

Taiwanese honor and obey their parents.
（台灣人尊敬並服從他們的父母。）
Taiwanese have strong family ties.
（台灣人有穩固的家族關係。）

honor ('anɚ) *v.* 尊敬　　obey (ə'be) *v.* 服從
strong (strɔŋ) *adj.* 穩固的　　ties (taɪz) *n. pl.* 關係

台灣人使用什麼語言？

What languages do Taiwanese use?

Taiwan's official language is
　Mandarin.

Southern Fujianese and Hakka are
　the main dialects.

The 12 aboriginal tribes all speak
　different languages.

＊＊

official〔ə'fɪʃəl〕*adj.* 官方的；正式的
Southern Fujianese 閩南語　　Hakka〔'hɑk'kɑ〕*n.* 客家話
Mandarin〔'mændərɪn〕*n.* 中國話；國語
main〔men〕*adj.* 主要的　　dialect〔'daɪəlɛkt〕*n.* 方言
aboriginal〔͵æbə'rɪdʒənḷ〕*adj.* 原住民的
tribe〔traɪb〕*n.* 部落

【背景說明】

1. ***What languages do Taiwanese use?***

這句話的意思是「台灣人都使用什麼語言？」也可以說：

What's the main language of Taiwan?
（台灣主要的語言是什麼？）
What language is spoken the most in Taiwan?
（台灣最常被使用的語言是什麼？）
What's the most popular language in Taiwan?
（台灣最普遍的語言是什麼？）
【main〔men〕*adj.* 主要的】

2. ***Taiwan's official language is Mandarin.***

official〔əˈfɪʃəl〕*adj.* 官方的；正式的
Mandarin〔ˈmændərɪn〕*n.* 中國話；國語

這句話的意思是「台灣的官方語言是國語。」
也可以說：

The government of Taiwan uses Mandarin.
（台灣政府使用國語。）
Mandarin is the accepted language of Taiwan.
（國語是為一般人所接納的台灣語言。）

government〔ˈgʌvənmənt〕*n.* 政府
accepted〔əkˈsɛptɪd〕*adj.* 為一般所接納的

3. ***Southern Fujianese and Hakka are the main dialects.***
   Southern Fujianese 閩南語　Hakka (ˈhɑkˈkɑ) *n.* 客家話
   Southern (ˈsʌðən) *adj.* 南方的　main (men) *adj.* 主要的
   dialect (ˈdaɪəlɛkt) *n.* 方言

   這句話的意思是「閩南語和客家話是主要的方言。」
   也可説成：

   Southern Fujianese and Hakka are the two
   　　dialects that are used most extensively.
   （閩南語和客家話是兩種被使用得最廣泛的方言。）
   Most Taiwanese can speak Southern
   　　Fujianese or Hakka.
   （大部分的台灣人會講閩南語或客家話。）

   【extensively (ɪkˈstɛnsɪvlɪ) *adv.* 廣泛地】

4. ***The 12 aboriginal tribes all speak different languages.***
   aboriginal (ˌæbəˈrɪdʒənl̩) *adj.* 原住民的
   tribe (traɪb) *n.* 部落

   這句話的意思是「十二個原住民部落都使用不同的
   語言。」也可説成：

   Each of the 12 aboriginal tribes has its own
   　　language.
   （十二個原住民部落，每一個都有自己的語言。）

Question
12 英文使用得很普遍嗎？

Is English spoken widely?

Many Taiwanese can speak a little English.

It's becoming increasingly popular.

It's now a mandatory subject in our school system.

**

widely (ˈwaɪdlɪ) *adv.* 廣泛地
increasingly (ɪnˈkrisɪŋlɪ) *adv.* 愈來愈
popular (ˈpɑpjələ) *adj.* 普遍的；流行的
mandatory (ˈmændəˌtorɪ) *adj.* 義務性的；強制的
subject (ˈsʌbdʒɪkt) *n.* 學科

【背景説明】

1. *Is English spoken widely?*

   widely (ˈwaɪdlɪ) *adv.* 廣泛地

   　　這句話的意思是「英文使用得很普遍嗎？」也可
   説成：

   > Do many people speak English?
   > （很多人說英文嗎？）
   > Is English spoken all over?
   > （到處都有人說英文嗎？）
   > 【 *all over* 到處… 】

2. *Many Taiwanese can speak a little English.*

   　　這句話的意思是「許多台灣人會說一點英文。」
   也可説成：

   > Most people in Taiwan speak a
   > little English.
   > （大部分的台灣人會說一點英文。）
   > Lots of Taiwanese can speak and
   > understand basic English.
   > （許多台灣人會說並懂得基本的英文。）
   > 【 *lots of* 許多 (= *many*)】

3. ***It's becoming increasingly popular.***
increasingly〔ɪnˈkrisɪŋlɪ〕*adv.* 愈來愈
popular〔ˈpɑpjələ〕*adj.* 普遍的；流行的

這句話的意思是「它漸漸變得普遍。」也可説成：

It's gaining popularity.（它愈來愈普遍。）
It's getting more popular every day.
（它一天比一天普遍。）
English is growing in popularity.
（英文變得愈來愈普遍。）

gain〔gen〕*v.* 增加
popularity〔ˌpɑpjəˈlærətɪ〕*n.* 普遍；流行
grow〔gro〕*v.* 成長

4. ***It's now a mandatory subject in our school system.***
mandatory〔ˈmændəˌtorɪ〕*adj.* 義務性的；強制的
subject〔ˈsʌbdʒɪkt〕*n.* 學科

這句話的意思是「它現在是我們學校制度中的一門
強制課程。」也可説成：

Taiwanese students must study English.
（台灣學生必須學英文。）
Every Taiwanese school teaches English.
（每一所台灣的學校都教英文。）
English class is mandatory for Taiwanese
students.（對台灣學生來說，英文課是強制課程。）

台灣的首都是哪裡？

What's the capital of Taiwan?

Taipei is Taiwan's political, economic and cultural center.

Taipei's diversity can satisfy everyone's needs.

Taipei is a vibrant international city.

**

capital ('kæpətl̩) *n.* 首都　　political (pə'lɪtɪkl̩) *adj.* 政治的
economic (,ikə'nɑmɪk) *adj.* 經濟的
cultural ('kʌltʃərəl) *adj.* 文化的
diversity (də'vɜsətɪ,daɪ-) *n.* 多樣性
satisfy ('sætɪs,faɪ) *v.* 滿足　　need (nid) *n.* 需求
vibrant ('vaɪbrənt) *adj.* 生氣勃勃的
international (,ɪntə'næʃənl̩) *adj.* 國際性的

【背景説明】

1. ***What's the capital of Taiwan?***

   capital (ˈkæpətl̩) *n.* 首都　*adj.* 首都的

   這句話的意思是「台灣的首都是哪裡？」也可説成：

   What's Taiwan's capital city?

   （台灣的首都是哪裡？）

   What's the capital city of Taiwan?

   （台灣的首都是哪裡？）

   Which city is Taiwan's capital?

   （哪個城市是台灣的首都？）

   capital 除表「首都」外，還可表「資金」、「大寫
   字母」；它也可當形容詞用，作「首都的」、「主要的」、
   「資金的」、「大寫的」等。

2. ***Taipei is Taiwan's political, economic and cultural
   center.***

   political (pəˈlɪtɪkl̩) *adj.* 政治的
   economic (ˌikəˈnamɪk) *adj.* 經濟的
   cultural (ˈkʌltʃərəl) *adj.* 文化的

   這句話的意思是「台北是台灣政治、經濟及文化的
   中心。」也可説成：

   Taipei is Taiwan's cosmopolitan center.

   （台北是台灣的國際中心。）

   【cosmopolitan (ˌkazməˈpalətn̩) *adj.* 世界性的；國際的】

3. ***Taipei's diversity can satisfy everyone's needs.***

diversity〔dəˈvɜsətɪ,daɪ-〕*n.* 多樣性

satisfy〔ˈsætɪsˌfaɪ〕*v.* 滿足　　need〔nid〕*n.* 需求

　　這句話的意思是「台北的多樣性能滿足每個人的需求。」也可以說：

> Taipei's diverse opportunities could
> 　satisfy anyone.
> （台北多樣的機會能滿足每一個人。）
> Taipei has something for everyone.
> （台北有每個人需要的東西。）
> 【opportunity〔ˌɑpəˈtjunətɪ〕*n.* 機會】

4. ***Taipei is a vibrant international city.***

vibrant〔ˈvaɪbrənt〕*adj.* 生氣勃勃的

international〔ˌɪntəˈnæʃənl̩〕*adj.* 國際性的

　　這句話的意思是「台北是一個生氣勃勃的國際性都市。」也可說成：

> Taipei is a lively city.
> （台北是個充滿活力的城市。）
> Taipei is a city on the go.
> （台北是一個忙碌的城市。）
> Taipei is full of life.（台北充滿了活力。）

lively〔ˈlaɪvlɪ〕*adj.* 充滿活力的
on the go 忙個不停的　　***be full of*** 充滿了～
life〔laɪf〕*n.* 活力

14 台灣政府的型態是什麼？

What type of government does Taiwan have?

Taiwan's government is a representative democracy.

The central government is divided into five branches.

There are four major political parties in Taiwan.

**

type〔taɪp〕*n.* 類型　government〔'gʌvənmənt〕*n.* 政府
representative〔ˌrɛprɪ'zɛntətɪv〕*adj.* 代議制的
democracy〔də'mɑkrəsɪ〕*n.* 民主政體；民主國家
be divided into 被分成　branch〔bræntʃ〕*n.* 部門
major〔'medʒə〕*adj.* 主要的　party〔'pɑrtɪ〕*n.* 黨派

【背景說明】

1. ***What type of government does Taiwan have?***

   type〔taɪp〕*n.* 類型　　government〔'gʌvənmənt〕*n.* 政府

   　　這句話的意思是「台灣政府的型態是什麼？」也可
   說成：What system of government does Taiwan
   have?（台灣政府的型態是什麼？）

   　　　句中的 system 也可代換成 form（型態）、style
   （種類；型式）或 kind（種類），意思不變。

2. ***Taiwan's government is a representative democracy.***

   representative〔ˌrɛprɪ'zɛntətɪv〕*adj.* 代議制的
   democracy〔də'mɑkrəsɪ〕*n.* 民主政體；民主國家

   　　這句話的意思是「台灣的政府是代議制的民主政
   體。」也可說成：

   Taiwan is a democracy.（台灣是一個民主國家。）
   Taiwan has a democratic government.

   （台灣有一個民主的政府。）

   【democratic〔ˌdɛmə'krætɪk〕*adj.* 民主的】

3. ***The central government is divided into five branches.***

   central〔'sɛntrəl〕*adj.* 中央的
   divide〔də'vaɪd〕*v.* 把⋯分爲
   be divided into 被分成　　branch〔bræntʃ〕*n.* 部門

   　　這句話的意思是「中央政府分爲五個部門。」也可
   說成：

Taiwan's government consists of five branches.

（台灣的政府是由五個部門組成。）

The Taiwan government has five distinct parts.

（台灣政府有五個不同的部門。）

這五個部門分別是行政院（Executive Yuan）、立法院（Legislative Yuan）、司法院（Judicial Yuan）、考試院（Examination Yuan）、監察院（Control Yuan）。

consist of 由~組成　distinct〔dɪ'stɪŋkt〕*adj.* 個別的；不同的
executive〔ɪg'zɛkjutɪv〕*adj.* 行政的
legislative〔'lɛdʒɪs,letɪv〕*adj.* 立法的
judicial〔dʒu'dɪʃəl〕*adj.* 司法的　control〔kən'trol〕*n.* 監督

4. *There are four major political parties in Taiwan.*

major〔'medʒɚ〕*adj.* 主要的　party〔'pɑrtɪ〕*n.* 黨派

這句話的意思是「台灣有四個主要的政黨。」

台灣四個主要的政黨分別是：民進黨（DPP/The Democratic Progressive Party）、國民黨（KMT/ The Kuomintang）、親民黨（PFP/ The People First Party），及台灣團結聯盟（TSU/Taiwan Solidarity Union）。

progressive〔prə'grɛsɪv〕*adj.* 進步的
Kuomintang〔'kwomɪn,tæŋ〕*n.* 國民黨
solidarity〔,sɑlə'dærətɪ〕*n.* 團結　union〔'junjən〕*n.* 聯盟

你們多久選一次總統？

How often do you vote for president?

We vote every four years.

Our president serves a four-year term.

Our voter turnout rate is very high.

**　**

vote〔vot〕v. 投票

president〔'prɛzədənt〕n. 總統

serve〔sɝv〕v. 任（職）　　term〔tɝm〕n. 任期

voter〔'votɚ〕n. 投票者

turnout〔'tɝn,aut〕n. 出席人（數）

voter turnout 投票人數　　rate〔ret〕n. 比率

【背景說明】

1. ***How often do you vote for president?***

   vote〔vot〕*v.* 投票
   president〔'prɛzədənt〕*n.* 總統

   　　這句話的意思是「你們多久選一次總統？」也可
   說成：

   > How often does Taiwan have a presidential
   > election?（台灣多久舉行一次總統選舉？）
   > How long is one term for your president?
   > （你們總統的任期多久？）

   　　often 是頻率副詞，表「經常地」，若想詢問事情發
   生的頻率時，可使用 "How often~?"「多久一次？」。

   presidential〔,prɛzə'dɛnʃəl〕*adj.* 總統的
   election〔ɪ'lɛkʃən〕*n.* 選舉

2. ***We vote every four years.***

   　　這句話的意思是「我們每四年投票一次。」也就是
   「我們每四年選一次。」也可說成：

   > We have elections every four years.
   > （我們每四年舉行一次選舉。）
   > Presidential elections are held every four years
   > in Taiwan.（台灣總統選舉每四年舉行一次。）

   　　【hold〔hold〕*v.* 舉行】

3. *Our president serves a four-year term.*

serve〔sɝv〕*v.* 任（職）   term〔tɝm〕*n.* 任期

這句話的意思是「我們的總統任期四年。」也可
說成：

One presidential term is four years.
（一個總統的任期是四年。）
Taiwan's president serves a four-year term.
（台灣總統四年一個任期。）

帶有數字的複數名詞當形容詞用時，必須變成
單數，如：a 10-**year**-old boy（一個十歲男孩），
a ten-**day** trip（一次十天的旅程）。

4. *The voter turnout rate is very high.*

voter〔'votɚ〕*n.* 投票者
turnout〔'tɝn,aʊt〕*n.* 出席人（數）
voter turnout 投票人數   rate〔ret〕*n.* 比率

這句話的意思是「（總統選舉的）投票率很高。」
也可說成：

In a presidential election, the polls are always high.
（在總統選舉時，投票數總是很高。）
Most Taiwanese vote in presidential elections.
（大部分的台灣人總統選舉時會去投票。）

【voting〔'votɪŋ〕*adj.* 投票的   poll〔pol〕*n.* 投票數】

16 教育體系怎麼樣？

---■

What's the educational system like?

Taiwan has nine years of compulsory education.

The elementary and secondary school system is excellent.

A competitive exam system keeps standards high.

**

compulsory (kəm'pʌlsərɪ) *adj.* 義務的；強制的
elementary (ˌɛlə'mɛntərɪ) *adj.* 初等的
secondary ('sɛkənˌdɛrɪ) *adj.* 中等的
excellent ('ɛkslᵊnt) *adj.* 極好的
competitive (kəm'pɛtətɪv) *adj.* 競爭激烈的
standard ('stændəd) *n.* 標準

【背景説明】

1. ***What's the educational system like?***

    這句話的意思是「教育體系怎麼樣？」也可説成：

    Tell me about Taiwan's educational system.

    (告訴我關於台灣的教育體系。)

    What's the school system in Taiwan like?

    (台灣的教育體系怎麼樣？)

2. ***Taiwan has nine years of compulsory education.***

    compulsory (kəm'pʌlsərɪ) *adj.* 義務的

    這句話的意思是「台灣有九年的義務教育。」也可
    説成：

    Taiwanese students must attend school for at
    least nine years. (台灣的學生必須上學至少九年。)

    All students must go to school for nine years
    in Taiwan. (台灣的學生必須上學九年。)

    【attend (ə'tɛnd) *v.* 上 (學)　***at least*** 至少 】

3. ***The elementary and secondary school system is excellent.***

    elementary (ˌɛlə'mɛntərɪ) *adj.* 初等的

    secondary ('sɛkənˌdɛrɪ) *adj.* 中等的

    這句話的意思是「台灣的初等及中等教育制度很
    棒。」也可説成：

The school system in Taiwan is superb.
（台灣的教育制度是極好的。）
Taiwan's school system is noted for its
excellence. （台灣的教育制度以它的卓越而聞名。）

superb〔su'pɝb〕*adj.* 極好的   noted〔'notɪd〕*adj.* 著名的
excellence〔'ɛksḷəns〕*n.* 卓越

　　台灣教育制度的各階段分別為：幼稚園
（kindergarten）、小學（elementary / primary
school）、國中（junior high school）、高中
（senior high school）、大學（university）、研
究所（graduate school）。

kindergarten〔'kɪndɚˌgɑrtṇ〕*n.* 幼稚園
primary〔'praɪˌmɛrɪ〕*adj.* 初級的   ***graduate school*** 研究所

4. ***A competitive exam system keeps standards high.***
competitive〔kəm'pɛtətɪv〕*adj.* 競爭激烈的
standard〔'stændɚd〕*n.* 標準

　　這句話字面的意思是「競爭激烈的考試制度一直維
持著高水準。」也就是「考試制度競爭激烈，而且一直
維持著很高的水準。」也可說成：

The exam system is competitive and standards
are high. （考試制度競爭激烈而且標準很高。）
Taiwan has a competitive and high quality exam
system. （台灣有競爭激烈而且優質的考試制度。）
【 ***high quality*** 優質的；高品質的 】

17　國旗是什麼樣子？

What does the flag look like?

Our flag has a red background.

It has a dark blue rectangle in the upper-left corner.

The blue rectangle bears a white sun with 12 triangular rays.

**

flag〔flæg〕*n.* 旗子【在此指「國旗」(national flag)】
background〔'bæk,graʊnd〕*n.* 背景；底色
rectangle〔'rɛktæŋgl〕*n.* 矩形；長方形
upper-left〔'ʌpɚ,lɛft〕*adj.* 左上方的
corner〔'kɔrnɚ〕*n.* 角落　　bear〔bɛr〕*v.* 帶有；具有
triangular〔traɪ'æŋgjəlɚ〕*adj.* 三角形的　　ray〔re〕*n.* 光線

【背景說明】

1. ***What does the flag look like?***
   flag〔flæg〕*n.* 旗子【在此指「國旗」(national flag)】

   這句話的意思是「國旗是什麼樣子？」也可說成：

   Describe the flag of Taiwan.

   （描述一下台灣的國旗。）

   What are the colors and features of Taiwan's flag?（台灣的國旗有什麼顏色和特色？）

   【describe〔dɪ'skraɪb〕*v.* 描述　feature〔'fitʃɚ〕*n.* 特色】

2. ***Our flag has a red background.***
   background〔'bæk͵graʊnd〕*n.* 背景；底色

   這句話的意思是「我們的國旗底色是紅色的。」也可說成：

   The flag's background is red.

   （國旗的底色是紅色的。）

   The flag is mostly red.（國旗的大部分是紅色的。）

3. ***It has a dark blue rectangle in the upper-left corner.***
   rectangle〔'rɛktæŋgl̩〕*n.* 矩形；長方形
   upper-left〔'ʌpɚ͵lɛft〕*adj.* 左上方的
   corner〔'kɔrnɚ〕*n.* 角落

   這句話的意思是「它的左上角有一個深藍色的長方形。」也可說成：

There's a dark blue rectangle on the upper-
　　left side. (左上方有一個深藍色的長方形。)

The flag has a dark blue square up in the left
　　corner. (國旗左上角有一個深藍色的方形。)

【square (skwɛr) *n.* 方形】

4. ***The blue rectangle bears a white sun with 12***
triangular rays.

bear (bɛr) *v.* 帶有；具有

triangular (traɪˈæŋgjələ) *adj.* 三角的　　ray (re) *n.* 光線

　　這句話的意思是「這藍色的長方形中，有一個十二
道三角光芒的白色太陽。」也可說成：

The rectangle contains a white sun with twelve
　　triangular rays.

(這長方形內，有一個十二道三角光芒的白色太陽。)

There's a white sun with twelve rays inside the
　　rectangle. (有一個十二道光芒的白色太陽在長方形裡。)

The rectangular area has a white sun with 12 rays
　　in it. (在長方形裡有一個十二道光芒的白色太陽。)

【contain (kənˈten) *v.* 含有】

　　bear 除了表「生 (孩子)」的意思外，也可表某人
或物「帶有；具有」武器、稱號、標記等，如：the
envelope bears a logo of the company (這信封上有
這家公司的標識)。【envelope (ˈɛnvəˌlop) *n.* 信封】

Question 18 台灣國旗的涵義是什麼？

> What's the significance of
> Taiwan's flag?

> The blue represents the sky,
>   symbolizing freedom.
>
> The white represents the sun,
>   symbolizing equality.
>
> The red represents blood,
>   symbolizing humanity.

**

significance (sɪg'nɪfəkəns) *n.* 涵義；意義
represent (,rɛprɪ'zɛnt) *v.* 代表
symbolize ('sɪmbḷ,aɪz) *v.* 象徵
freedom ('fridəm) *n.* 自由　　equality (ɪ'kwɑlətɪ) *n.* 平等
blood (blʌd) *n.* 血　　humanity (hju'mænətɪ) *n.* 博愛

【背景說明】

1. *What's the significance of Taiwan's flag?*
   significance〔 sɪgˋnɪfəkəns 〕*n.* 涵義；意義

   這句話的意思是「台灣國旗的涵義是什麼？」也
   可說成：

   What do the flag's symbols and colors mean?
   （國旗上的符號和顏色有什麼涵義？）
   What do the flag's features represent?
   （國旗的特徵代表什麼？）

   symbol〔ˋsɪmbl 〕*n.* 符號　　feature〔ˋfitʃɚ 〕*n.* 特徵；特色
   represent〔ˏrɛprɪˋzɛnt 〕*v.* 代表

2. *The blue represents the sky, symbolizing freedom.*
   represent〔ˏrɛprɪˋzɛnt 〕*v.* 代表
   symbolize〔ˋsɪmblˏaɪz 〕*v.* 象徵
   freedom〔ˋfridəm 〕*n.* 自由

   這句話的意思是「藍色代表天空，象徵自由。」
   也可說成：

   The blue part is the sky, which means freedom.
   （藍色的部分是天空，表示自由。）
   The flag's blue represents the sky and freedom.
   （國旗的藍色代表天空和自由。）
   The blue also represents democracy.
   （藍色也代表民主主義。）
   【democracy〔 dəˋmɑkrəsɪ 〕*n.* 民主主義】

3. ***The white represents the sun**, symbolizing equality.*

equality〔ɪ'kwɑlətɪ〕*n.* 平等

這句話的意思是「白色代表太陽，象徵平等。」
也可說成：

The white shape is the sun, which represents
　　equality. (白色的形狀是太陽，代表平等。)
The white also represents people's livelihood.
(白色也代表民生主義。)

shape〔ʃep〕*n.* 形狀
livelihood〔'laɪvlɪˌhʊd〕*n.* 生活；生計

4. ***The red represents blood**, symbolizing humanity.*

blood〔blʌd〕*n.* 血
humanity〔hju'mænətɪ〕*n.* 博愛

這句話的意思是「紅色代表血液，象徵博愛。」
也可說成：

The red symbolizes blood and humanity.
(紅色象徵血液和博愛。)
The red on the flag means blood and humanity.
(國旗上的紅色表示血液和博愛。)
The red also represents nationalism.
(紅色也代表民族主義。)

【nationalism〔'næʃənḷˌɪzəm〕*n.* 民族主義】

台灣的氣候如何？

What's Taiwan's climate like?

Taiwan has two main seasons.

Summer is usually hot and humid.

Winter can be mild, chilly and wet.

** ─────────────

climate ('klaımıt) *n.* 氣候

main (men) *adj.* 主要的   season ('sizn) *n.* 季節

humid ('hjumıd) *adj.* 潮濕的

mild (maıld) *adj.* 溫和的；溫暖的

chilly ('tʃılı) *adj.* 寒冷的   wet (wɛt) *adj.* 潮濕的

【背景說明】

1. ***What's Taiwan's climate like?***

   climate〔'klaɪmɪt〕 *n.* 氣候

   這句話的意思是「台灣的氣候如何？」也可說成：

   What is the climate like in Taiwan?
   （台灣的氣候怎麼樣？）

   What's the weather like in Taiwan?
   （台灣的天氣如何？）

   How is the weather in Taiwan?
   (= What is the weather in Taiwan like?)
   （台灣的天氣如何？）

   climate（氣候）是指某個地方一整年氣候的大
   致狀況，而 weather（天氣）通常是指特定地方在特
   定時間天氣的情況。

2. ***Taiwan has two main seasons.***

   main〔men〕 *adj.* 主要的　　season〔'sizn̩〕 *n.* 季節

   這句話的意思是「台灣有兩個主要的季節。」也
   可說成：There are two main seasons in Taiwan.
   （在台灣有兩個主要的季節。）

   台灣四季的氣候變化並不明顯，春天（spring）
   和秋天（fall）持續的時間不長，所以感覺上好像只
   有夏天和冬天。

3. *Summer is usually hot and humid.*

humid〔'hjumɪd〕*adj.* 潮濕的

　　這句話的意思是「夏天通常炎熱而且潮濕。」也可說成：

Taiwan's summer is normally hot and damp.
（台灣的夏天通常炎熱而且潮濕。）

Summers in Taiwan are really hot and there is high humidity.
（台灣的夏天真的很熱，而且濕度很高。）

normally〔'nɔrmlɪ〕*adv.* 通常　　damp〔dæmp〕*adj.* 潮濕的
humidity〔hju'mɪdətɪ〕*n.* 濕氣

　　moist 也是表「潮濕的」，但它一般不用於形容天氣，如：moist foods（含水分的食物／濕的食物）、a moist wipe（一條濕的抹布）。

【moist〔mɔɪst〕*adj.* 微濕的　　wipe〔'waɪp〕*n.* 抹布】

4. *Winter can be mild, chilly and wet.*

mild〔maɪld〕*adj.* 溫和的；溫暖的
chilly〔'tʃɪlɪ〕*adj.* 寒冷的　　wet〔wɛt〕*adj.* 潮濕的

　　這句話的意思是「冬天可能是溫和、寒冷而且潮濕。」也可說成：Winter is a colder and wetter season.（冬天是一個比較寒冷而且比較潮濕的季節。）

　　表示「可能性或推測」時，可用 can，表「可能…」，否定時用 cannot「不可能」。

台灣有雨季嗎？

Does Taiwan have a rainy season?

Taiwan's rainy season is around the end of May.

People call these rains the plum rains.

It is said that these rains cause the plums to swell and ripen.

**

rainy ('renɪ) *adj.* 多雨的；下雨的

season ('sizn̩) *n.* 季節

around (ə'raʊnd) *prep.* 大約；差不多

plum (plʌm) *n.* 梅子　***plum rains*** 梅雨

cause (kɔz) *v.* 造成　swell (swɛl) *v.* 變大

ripen ('raɪpən) *v.* 成熟

【背景說明】

1. *Does Taiwan have a rainy season?*
   rainy (ˈrenɪ) *adj.* 多雨的；下雨的
   season (ˈsizn̩) *n.* 季節；時期

> 這句話的意思是「台灣有雨季嗎？」也可說成：
>
> Is there a rainy season in Taiwan?
>
> （台灣有雨季嗎？）
>
> Does Taiwan have a season when it rains a lot?
>
> （台灣有常常下雨的時期嗎？）

> season 不只是表四季，也可指在某一固定期間內會循環發生的事，如：the baseball season（棒球季）、the mango season（芒果季）、the tuna season（鮪魚季）。【mango (ˈmæŋgo) *n.* 芒果　tuna (ˈtunə) *n.* 鮪魚】

2. *Taiwan's rainy season is around the end of May.*
   around (əˈraʊnd) *prep.* 大約；差不多

> 這句話的意思是「台灣的雨季通常在五月下旬左右。」也可以說：
>
> In Taiwan, it rains a lot in late May.
>
> （在台灣，五月下旬常下雨。）
>
> Taiwan's wet season is around late May
>   and early June.
>
> （台灣的雨季在五月下旬到六月上旬左右。）
>
> late (let) *adj.* 後期的；末期的　early (ˈɝlɪ) *adj.* 初期的
> wet (wɛt) *adj.* （下）雨的；多雨的

3. ***People call these rains the plum rains.***

plum〔plʌm〕*n.* 梅子　　***plum rains*** 梅雨

　　　這句話的意思是「人們稱這種雨爲梅雨。」也可
説成：

The rains are called "plum rains."

（這種雨被稱爲「梅雨」。）

Many refer to these rains as "the plum rains."

（許多人稱這些雨爲「梅雨」。）

Taiwanese like to call these rains "plum rains."

（台灣人喜歡稱這些雨爲「梅雨」。）

【*refer to⋯as~*　稱⋯爲~ 】

4. ***It is said that these rains cause the plums to swell
and ripen.***

it is said that~ 聽說~　　cause〔kɔz〕*v.* 造成
swell〔swɛl〕*v.* 變大　　ripen〔'raɪpən〕*v.* 成熟

　　　這句話的意思是「據說那些雨會使梅子變大、變成
熟。」也可説成：

People say that "plum rains" ripen
　　and enlarge the plums.

（據說「梅雨」使梅子變成熟並且變大。）

enlarge〔ɪn'lɑrdʒ〕*v.* 使變大

颱風季節是什麼時候？

When is the typhoon season?

Typhoons usually occur in summer, especially in July and August.

In the early fall, one sti!l might encounter typhoons.

Typhoons usually bring powerful winds and heavy rains.

＊＊

typhoon (taɪˋfun) *n.* 颱風　occur (əˋkɝ) *v.* 發生
fall (fɔl) *n.* 秋天　encounter (ɪnˋkaʊntɚ) *v.* 遭遇
powerful (ˋpaʊəfəl) *adj.* 強有力的
heavy (ˋhɛvɪ) *adj.* 大量的

【背景説明】

1. ***When is the typhoon season?***

   typhoon〔taɪˋfun〕*n.* 颱風

   　　這句話的意思是「颱風季節是什麼時候？」也可以說：

   When is the season for typhoons in Taiwan?

   （台灣的颱風季節是什麼時候？）

   When do typhoons usually hit Taiwan?

   （颱風通常什麼時候會侵襲台灣？）

   【hit〔hɪt〕*v.* 侵襲】

2. ***Typhoons usually occur in summer, especially in July and August.***

   occur〔əˋkɝ〕*v.* 發生

   　　這句話的意思是「颱風通常發生在夏天，尤其是在七、八月。」也可說成：

   Summer is Taiwan's typhoon season.

   （夏天是台灣的颱風季節。）

   Most typhoons usually hit Taiwan in July,
   　　August or late summer.

   （大部分的颱風通常在七、八月或夏末侵襲台灣。）

   　　occur 和 happen 雖然都是指「發生」，但通常天然災害的發生，都用 occur。

3. ***In the early fall, one still might encounter typhoons.***

early (ˈɝlɪ) *adj.* 初期的　　fall (fɔl) *n.* 秋天

encounter (ɪnˈkaʊntɚ) *v.* 遭遇

　　這句話的意思是「在初秋，仍然有可能會遇到颱風。」也可說成：

Typhoons are also possible in early autumn.

（初秋也有可能有颱風。）

Sometimes, in September, a typhoon might hit.

（九月有時也可能有颱風侵襲。）

【autumn (ˈɔrtəm) *n.* 秋天】

　　encounter 除了指「遭遇（困難或危險）」（主詞可以是人或物）外，也可指「偶遇、邂逅（某人）」。

4. ***Typhoons usually bring powerful winds and heavy rains.***

powerful (ˈpaʊɚfəl) *adj.* 有力的

heavy (ˈhɛvɪ) *adj.* 大量的

　　這句話的意思是「颱風通常會帶來強風和豪雨。」也可說成：

Most typhoons are powerful with big winds
　　and heavy rains.

（大部分的颱風都很強，會挾帶強風和豪雨。）

Powerful winds and rains accompany most
　　typhoons. （大部分的颱風都伴隨著強大的風雨。）

【accompany (əˈkʌmpənɪ) *v.* 伴隨】

台灣有很多山嗎？

Is Taiwan mountainous?

More than two-thirds of the island is covered with mountains.

The Central Range bisects the island from north to south.

The tallest is Jade Mountain at 3952 m.

**

mountainous (ˈmauntn̩əs) *adj.* 多山的；山地的
two-thirds 三分之二　　cover (ˈkʌvɚ) *v.* 覆蓋
range (rendʒ) *n.* 山脈　***the Central Range*** 中央山脈
bisect (baɪˈsɛkt) *v.* 把…一分為二
jade (dʒed) *n.* 玉

【背景説明】

1. *Is Taiwan mountainous?*

   mountainous (ˈmaʊntṇəs) *adj.* 多山的

   　　這句話的意思是「台灣有很多山嗎？」也可説成：

   Are there lots of mountains in Taiwan?

   （台灣有很多山嗎？）

   Does Taiwan have a lot of mountains?

   （台灣有很多山嗎？）

2. *More than two-thirds of the island is covered with mountains.*

   cover (ˈkʌvɚ) *v.* 覆蓋

   　　這句話的意思是「這座島有超過三分之二的地區被山所覆蓋。」也就是「台灣有三分之二的地區是山。」也可以説：

   Most of Taiwan is covered with mountains.

   （台灣大部分的地區都被山所覆蓋。）

   More than sixty-five percent of Taiwan is mountainous. （台灣百分之六十五以上的地區是山。）

3. *The Central Range bisects the island from north to south.*

   range (rendʒ) *n.* 山脈　　　*the Central Range* 中央山脈

   bisect (baɪˈsɛkt) *v.* 把…一分爲二

   　　這句話的意思是「中央山脈把這座島從北到南一分爲二。」也可説成：

The Central Mountain Range, which runs from north to south, cuts Taiwan in two.
（南北走向的中央山脈把台灣分割成兩半。）

Taiwan is divided into two parts by the north-south Central Mountain Range.
（台灣被南北走向的中央山脈分成兩個部分。）

【divide〔də'vaɪd〕*v.* 劃分　*be divided into* 被分成～】

4. *The tallest is Jade Mountain at 3952 m.*

jade〔dʒed〕*n.* 玉
Jade Mountain 玉山（= *Mt. Jade*）

這句話的意思是「最高的山是 3952 公尺的玉山。」也可説成：

Taiwan's tallest mountain is Jade Mountain.
（台灣最高的山是玉山。）

At 3952 meters, Jade Mountain is Taiwan's tallest.
（3952 公尺高的玉山，是台灣最高的山。）

【meter〔'mitæ〕*n.* 公尺】

at 這個介系詞除可用來表時間，如 at five o'clock，亦可用來表「速度」、「高度」，或「溫度」。

經濟狀況如何？

How's the economy doing?

Current trends show steady growth.

Taiwan has a dynamic business spirit.

We're still an innovative power and leading producer.

**

economy (ɪ'kɑnəmɪ) *n.* 經濟　do (du) *v.* 進展
current ('kɝənt) *adj.* 目前的　trend (trɛnd) *n.* 趨勢
steady ('stɛdɪ) *adj.* 穩定的　growth (groθ) *n.* 成長
dynamic (daɪ'næmɪk) *adj.* 有活力的
spirit ('spɪrɪt) *n.* 精神　innovative ('ɪnəˌvetɪv) *adj.* 創新的
leading ('lidɪŋ) *adj.* 一流的；主要的
producer (prə'djusɚ) *n.* 生產者

【背景說明】

1. *How's the economy doing?*

economy〔ɪˋkɑnəmɪ〕*n.* 經濟　　do〔du〕*v.* 進展

這句話的意思是「經濟狀況如何？」也可說成：

How is Taiwan's economy?（台灣的經濟如何？）
What's Taiwan's current economic situation?
（台灣目前的經濟狀況如何？）

current〔ˋkɝənt〕*adj.* 目前的
economic〔͵ikəˋnɑmɪk〕*adj.* 經濟的
situation〔͵sɪtʃʊˋeʃən〕*n.* 情況

do 在這裡是表「事情進展的情況」，它也可表
「人的狀況」，如：How are you doing?（你最近
怎麼樣？）、How do you do?（你好嗎？）等。

2. *Current trends show steady growth.*

current〔ˋkɝənt〕*adj.* 目前的　　trend〔trɛnd〕*n.* 趨勢
steady〔ˋstɛdɪ〕*adj.* 穩定的　　growth〔groθ〕*n.* 成長

這句話的意思是「目前的趨勢呈現穩定的成長。」
也可說成：

Current signs show a steady growth.
（目前的跡象呈現穩定的成長。）
Current trends show gradual improvement.
（目前趨勢呈現逐漸改善的跡象。）

sign〔saɪn〕*n.* 跡象；徵兆　　gradual〔ˋgrædʒʊəl〕*adj.* 逐漸的
improvement〔ɪmˋpruvmənt〕*n.* 改善

3. ***Taiwan has a dynamic business spirit.***

dynamic〔daɪ'næmɪk〕*adj.* 有活力的

spirit〔'spɪrɪt〕*n.* 精神

這句話的意思是「台灣有充滿活力的企業精神。」

也可說成：

Taiwanese are dynamic business people.

（台灣人是充滿活力的生意人。）

The business climate in Taiwan is very dynamic.

（在台灣，商業的風氣非常活躍。）

Taiwan is a dynamic place in terms of business.

（就商業的角度，台灣是一個充滿活力的地方。）

climate〔'klaɪmɪt〕*n.* 風氣

in terms of 以…的角度；從…的觀點

4. ***We're still an innovative power and leading producer.***

innovative〔'ɪnə,vetɪv〕*adj.* 創新的

power〔'pauɚ〕*n.* 強國；大國

leading〔'lidɪŋ〕*adj.* 一流的；主要的

producer〔prə'djusɚ〕*n.* 生產者

這句話的意思是「我們仍然是一個創新的強國和一流的生產者。」也可說成：

Taiwan is still an innovative and productive country.（台灣仍然是一個創新和多產的國家。）

productive〔prə'dʌktɪv〕*adj.* 有生產力的；多產的

24 什麼是台灣主要的產業？

What's Taiwan's main industry?

Taiwan is a high-tech giant.

The electronic industries are
    booming.

Taiwan is a world leader in computers
    and semiconductors.

**

industry ('ɪndəstrɪ) *n.* 產業；工業
high-tech 高科技【tech 是 technology 的簡寫】
giant ('dʒaɪənt) *n.* 巨人
electronic (ɪ,lɛk'trɑnɪk) *adj.* 電子的
boom (bum) *v.* 突然繁榮起來
semiconductor (,sɛməkən'dʌktə) *n.* 半導體

【背景說明】

1. ***What's Taiwan's main industry?***

   main〔men〕*adj.* 主要的　　industry〔'ɪndəstrɪ〕*n.* 產業

   這句話的意思是「什麼是台灣主要的產業？」也
   可說成：

   What's the main industry in Taiwan?
   （什麼是台灣主要的產業？）

   In terms of importance, what is Taiwan's
   main industry?
   （從重要性的角度來看，什麼是台灣主要的產業？）
   【*in terms of* 以…的角度】

2. ***Taiwan is a high-tech giant.***

   high-tech〔'haɪ,tɛk〕*adj.* 高科技的
   giant〔'dʒaɪənt〕*n.* 巨人；巨物

   這句話字面的意思是「台灣是高科技的巨人。」也
   就是「台灣是高科技的強國。」也可說成：

   Taiwan is a high-tech super power.
   （台灣是高科技的超級大國。）
   Taiwan is a global leader in high technology.
   （台灣是全球高科技的領導者。）
   Taiwan has an excellent reputation as a high-tech
   manufacturer. （台灣是享有最高聲譽的高科技製造者。）

   global〔'globl〕*adj.* 全球的　　technology〔tɛk'nɑlədʒɪ〕*n.* 科技
   excellent〔'ɛkslənt〕*adj.* 極好的　　reputation〔,rɛpjə'teʃən〕*n.* 名聲
   manufacturer〔,mænjə'fæktʃərə〕*n.* 製造商

3. *The electronic industries are booming.*

electronic〔ɪˌlɛk'trɑnɪk〕*adj.* 電子的

boom〔bum〕*v.* 突然繁榮起來；迅速發展

　　這句話的意思是「電子產業日趨繁榮。」也可說成：

Taiwan's electronic industry is thriving.

（台灣的電子產業很繁榮。）

The electronic industry in Taiwan is flourishing.

（電子產業在台灣很繁榮。）

【thrive〔θraɪv〕*v.* 繁榮；興盛　flourish〔'flɝɪʃ〕*v.* 繁榮；興盛】

　　boom、thrive、flourish 都有繁榮的意思，但
boom 含有「突然」繁榮的意味。

4. *Taiwan is a world leader in computers and*
semiconductors.

semiconductor〔ˌsɛməkən'dʌktɚ〕*n.* 半導體

　　這句話的意思是「台灣在電腦和半導體上是世界的
領導者。」也可說成：

Taiwan is a leading producer of computers
and semiconductors.

（台灣是電腦和半導體一流的生產者。）

　　semiconductor 也可以 semi-conductor 的形
式表現。semi 加在名詞或形容詞之前，表示「半…；
稍微…」，除了專有名詞及 i 開頭的字外，通常不加連
字號。

台灣的農業如何？

> **How's Taiwan's agriculture?**

> Rice and tea are major crops.
>
> Sugar cane and a variety of fruits are also important.
>
> Hog, poultry and shrimp farms are popular, too.

** ─────────────

agriculture (ˈægrɪ͵kʌltʃɚ) *n.* 農業
rice (raɪs) *n.* 稻米　major (ˈmedʒɚ) *adj.* 主要的
crop (krɑp) *n.* 農作物　***sugar cane*** 甘蔗
variety (vəˈraɪətɪ) *n.* 多樣性　***a variety of*** 各種的
hog (hɑg) *n.* 豬　poultry (ˈpoltrɪ) *n.* 家禽
shrimp (ʃrɪmp) *n.* 蝦子　farm (fɑrm) *n.* 養殖場
popular (ˈpɑpjələ) *adj.* 普遍的

【背景説明】

1. ***How's Taiwan's agriculture?***

   agriculture (ˈægrɪˌkʌltʃə) *n.* 農業

   > 這句話的意思是「台灣的農業如何？」也可説成：

   Please tell me about Taiwan's agricultural
   industry. (請告訴我關於台灣的農業。)

   What are the main farming products in Taiwan?
   (什麼是台灣主要的農產品？)

   > agricultural (ˌægrɪˈkʌltʃərəl) *adj.* 農業的
   > farming (ˈfɑrmɪŋ) *adj.* 農業的　　product (ˈprɑdʌkt) *n.* 產品

2. ***Rice and tea are major crops.***

   rice (raɪs) *n.* 稻米　　major (ˈmedʒə) *adj.* 主要的
   crop (krɑp) *n.* 農作物

   > 這句話的意思是「稻米和茶葉是主要的農作物。」
   > 也可説成：Rice and tea are two main agricultural
   > products. (稻米和茶葉是兩種主要的農產品。)

3. ***Sugar cane and a variety of fruits are also important.***

   sugar (ˈʃʊgə) *n.* 糖　　cane (ken) *n.* 莖 (長且有節)
   sugar cane 甘蔗　　variety (vəˈraɪətɪ) *n.* 種類；多樣性
   a variety of 各種的

   > 這句話的意思是「甘蔗和各式各樣的水果也很重
   > 要。」也可説成：

Fruits and sugar cane are also important
products. (水果和甘蔗也是重要的產物。)

Taiwan farmers also have great success with
fruits and sugar cane.

(台灣的農夫在種植水果和甘蔗上，也有很好的成果。)

farmer ('fɑrmɚ) *n.* 農人　success (sək'sɛs) *n.* 成功；好結果

4. *Hog, poultry and shrimp farms are popular, too.*

hog (hɑg) *n.* 豬　poultry ('poltrɪ) *n.* 家禽
shrimp (ʃrɪmp) *n.* 蝦子　farm (fɑrm) *n.* 養殖場
popular ('pɑpjələ) *adj.* 普遍的

　　這句話的意思是「豬、家禽和蝦子的養殖場也很
普遍。」也可說成：

Taiwan's pork, chicken and seafood products
are also good moneymakers.

(台灣的豬肉、雞肉和海鮮產品，也是很賺錢的事業。)

Popular products also include pork, poultry
and seafood.

(普遍的產物也包括了豬肉、家禽和海鮮。)

【 pork (pork) *n.* 豬肉　seafood ('si,fud) *n.* 海鮮 】

　　農業不只是指種植作物，畜牧養殖也包含在農業
內。句中的 hog 也可用 pig 代替，hog 通常指的是人
工飼養的肉豬，豬肉是 pork；雞和雞肉都是用 chicken
這個字；牛是 cattle，牛肉則是 beef。

【 cattle ('kætl̩) *n.* 牛；家畜　beef (bif) *n.* 牛肉 】

Question 26 台灣曾經被殖民嗎？

Was Taiwan ever colonized?

Foreign powers have tried to rule Taiwan.

The Spanish and Dutch occupied parts of it in the 17th century.

Taiwan was ceded to Japan as a result of the Sino-Japanese War.

**

colonize ('kɑlə,naɪz) v. 開拓…成殖民地；殖民
foreign ('fɔrɪn) adj. 外來的　power ('pauɚ) n. 強國
rule (rul) v. 統治　*the Spanish* 西班牙人
the Dutch 荷蘭人　occupy ('ɑkjə,paɪ) v. 佔領
cede (sid) v. 割讓
Sino- (,saɪno-) 中國的；中國與…的（複合用詞）

【背景説明】

1. ***Was Taiwan ever colonized?***

   ever (ˈɛvɚ) *adv.* 曾經

   colonize (ˈkɑləˌnaɪz) *v.* 開拓…成殖民地；殖民

   　　這句話的意思是「台灣曾經被殖民嗎？」也可説成：

   Was Taiwan ever a colony? (台灣曾經是殖民地嗎？)

   Did any other countries ever colonize Taiwan?

   (曾經有別的國家殖民過台灣嗎？)

   【colony (ˈkɑlənɪ) *n.* 殖民地】

2. ***Foreign powers have tried to rule Taiwan.***

   foreign (ˈfɔrɪn) *adj.* 外國的　　powers (ˈpauɚz) *n. pl.* 強國

   rule (rul) *v.* 統治

   　　這句話的意思是「外國強權曾經試圖統治台灣。」

   也可説成：Several countries have tried to colonize

   Taiwan. (有好幾個國家試圖殖民台灣。)

   　　power 除了表「力量；權力」，也可表具有強大影

   響力的國家或組織。

3. ***The Spanish and Dutch occupied parts of it in the 17th***
   century.

   the Spanish 西班牙人　　***the Dutch*** 荷蘭人

   occupy (ˈɑkjəˌpaɪ) *v.* 佔領　　century (ˈsɛntʃərɪ) *n.* 世紀

   　　這句話的意思是「在十七世紀時，西班牙人和荷蘭

   人佔領了部分的台灣。」也可説成：

Parts of Taiwan were briefly controlled by
　　the Spanish and the Dutch.

（台灣有些部分曾短暫地被西班牙人和荷蘭人統治過。）

The Spanish and the Dutch briefly controlled
　　parts of Taiwan.

（西班牙人和荷蘭人曾短暫地控制部分的台灣。）

　　briefly〔'briflɪ〕*adv.* 短暫地　　control〔kən'trol〕*v.* 管理；支配

　　　因為 Spanish（西班牙人的）和 Dutch（荷蘭人的）
是形容詞，在前面加上 the，可當複數名詞用；它們的
單數可數名詞分別為 Spaniard〔'spænjəd〕*n.* 西班牙人
和 Dutchman〔'dʌtʃmən〕*n.* 荷蘭人。

4. ***Taiwan was ceded to Japan as a result of the***
　　Sino-Japanese War.
cede〔sid〕*v.* 割讓
Sino-〔ˌsaɪno-〕中國的；中國與…的（複合用詞）

　　　這句話的意思是「台灣被割讓給日本，是中日戰爭
的結果。」也可說成：

Taiwan was given to Japan as a result of
　　the war.（台灣被送給日本是戰爭的結果。）

Japan gained control of Taiwan as a war prize.
　　（日本取得台灣的控制權，當作是戰爭的獎賞。）

Japan got control of Taiwan as a result of
　　winning the Sino-Japanese War.
　　（日本取得台灣的控制權，是中日戰爭勝利的結果。）

哪個殖民國影響台灣最深？

Which colonizer influenced Taiwan most?

The Japanese modernized Taiwan's agriculture and transportation.

They forcibly suppressed the language and customs of Taiwan.

Fifty years of Japanese colonialism greatly affected Taiwan.

**

colonizer〔ˋkɑləˏnaɪzɚ〕n. 開拓殖民地的國家
modernize〔ˋmɑdɚnˏaɪz〕v. 使現代化
transportation〔ˏtrænspɚˋteʃən〕n. 交通運輸
forcibly〔ˋforsəblɪ〕adv. 強制性地
suppress〔səˋprɛs〕v. 壓制　custom〔ˋkʌstəm〕n. 習俗
colonialism〔kəˋlonɪəlˏɪzəm〕n. 殖民政策

【背景説明】

1. ***Which colonizer influenced Taiwan most?***

   colonizer (ˈkɑləˌnaɪzɚ) *n.* 開拓殖民地的國家

   influence (ˈɪnfluəns) *v.* 影響

   　　這句話的意思是「哪個殖民國影響台灣最深？」

   也可説成：

   > Which ruling power influenced Taiwan the
   > most? (哪一個統治國影響台灣最深？)
   > Which foreign country affected Taiwan more?
   > (哪一個外來的國家對台灣的影響比較深？)

   【ruling (ˈrulɪŋ) *adj.* 統治的　power (ˈpauɚ) *adj.* 權力；強國】

2. ***The Japanese modernized Taiwan's agriculture
   and transportation.***

   modernize (ˈmɑdɚnˌaɪz) *v.* 使現代化

   transportation (ˌtrænspɚˈteʃən) *n.* 交通運輸

   　　這句話的意思是「日本人使台灣的農業和交通運

   輸現代化。」也可説成：

   > The Japanese helped modernize Taiwan in
   > many ways.
   > (日本人在很多方面幫助台灣現代化。)
   > Japan really improved Taiwan's farming
   > and transportation.
   > (日本確實改善了台灣的農業和交通運輸。)

   improve (ɪmˈpruv) *v.* 改善　farming (ˈfɑrmɪŋ) *n.* 農業

3. ***They forcibly suppressed the language and customs
of Taiwan.***

forcibly〔'fɔrsəblɪ〕*adv.* 強制地　suppress〔sə'prɛs〕*v.* 壓制
custom〔'kʌstəm〕*n.* 習俗

　　這句話的意思是「他們強制地壓制台灣的語言和風
俗。」也可説成：

> The Japanese limited or abolished many of
> Taiwan's customs.
> （日本人限制並廢除許多台灣的風俗。）

> The Japanese used force to limits the Taiwanese
> culture.（日本人使用武力限制台灣的文化。）

　　【limit〔'lɪmɪt〕*v.* 限制　abolish〔ə'bɑlɪʃ〕*v.* 廢除】

　　suppress 也可表示「忍住；抑制」情緒表現、呵欠等，
如：suppress a smile（忍住微笑）、suppress *one's* sobs
（忍住啜泣）、The pill can suppress a cough.（這藥可抑
制咳嗽。）等。【sob〔sɑb〕*n.* 啜泣　pill〔pɪl〕*n.* 藥丸】

4. ***Fifty years of Japanese colonialism greatly affected
Taiwan.***

colonialism〔kə'lonɪəl‚ɪzəm〕*n.* 殖民政策
affect〔ə'fɛkt〕*v.* 影響（= *influence*）

　　這句話的意思是「五十年的日本殖民政策對台灣造
成很大的影響。」也可説成：The Japanese occupation
of Taiwan had a great influence on Taiwan.（日本
佔領台灣，對台灣有很大的影響。）

　　【occupation〔‚ɑkjə'peʃən〕*n.* 佔領　influence〔'ɪnflʊəns〕*n.* 影響】

28 一百元鈔票上的照片是誰？

Whose picture is on the 100-dollar bill?

It's Sun Yat-sen's, the Founding
Father of the R.O.C.

He led the overthrow of the inept
Manchu government.

He developed the "Three Principles
of the People."

**

bill〔 bɪl 〕*n.* 鈔票　*Founding Father* 創始人
lead〔 lid 〕*v.* 領導　overthrow〔'ovɚ͵θro 〕*n.* 推翻
inept〔 ɪn'ɛpt 〕*adj.* 無能的
Manchu〔 mæn'tʃu 〕*adj.* 滿洲的
develop〔 dɪ'vɛləp 〕*v.* 培養；開發
Three Principles of the People 三民主義

【背景說明】

1. **Whose picture is on the 100-dollar bill?**
   bill〔bɪl〕*n.* 鈔票

   這句話的意思是「一百元鈔票上的照片是誰？」
   也可說成：

   Who is the man with his picture on the
   100-dollar bill? (一百元鈔票上的那個人是誰？)
   Who is the guy on the New Taiwan 100-dollar bill?
   (一百元新台幣上的那個人是誰？)【guy〔gaɪ〕*n.* 傢伙；人】

2. **It's Sun Yat-sen's, the Founding Father of the R.O.C.**
   found〔faʊnd〕*v.* 創立
   the R.O.C. 中華民國 (= *the Republic of China*)

   這句話的意思是「是孫逸仙（孫中山）的照片，
   他是中華民國的國父。」也可說成：

   The picture is of Dr. Sun Yat-sen, the
   "Father of the ROC."
   (是孫逸仙博士的照片，他是「中華民國的國父」。)
   The man is Dr. Sun Yat-sen, the founder
   of modern China.
   (那個人是孫逸仙博士，他是現代中國的創立者。)
   【founder〔'faʊndɚ〕*n.* 創立者】

   found 在這裡不是 find 的過去式或過去分詞，而
   是作「創立；建立」解。

3. *He led the overthrow of the inept Manchu government.*

lead〔lid〕*v.* 領導　　overthrow〔'ovɚ͵θro〕*n.,v.* 推翻

inept〔ɪn'ɛpt〕*adj.* 無能的　　Manchu〔mæn'tʃu〕*adj.* 滿洲的

　　　　這句話的意思是「他領導推翻無能的滿清政府。」
也可説成：

He is responsible for overthrowing the Manchu
government. (他肩負起推翻滿清政府的責任。)

Dr. Sun led the revolution to overthrow the
Manchu government.

(孫博士領導革命，推翻了滿清政府。)

responsible〔rɪ'spɑnsəbl̩〕*adj.* 負起⋯責任的
revolution〔͵rɛvə'luʃən〕*n.* 革命

4. *He developed the "Three Principles of the People."*

develop〔dɪ'vɛləp〕*v.* 培養；開發

　　　　這句話的意思是「他建構了三民主義。」也可説成：

He started the "Three Principles of the People"
idea for the Chinese.

(他爲中國人創立三民主義的思想。)

He introduced the concept of the "Three
Principles of the People."

(他推廣「三民主義」的思想。)

introduce〔͵ɪntrə'djus〕*v.* 推廣　　start〔stɑrt〕*v.* 創始
concept〔'kɑnsɛpt〕*n.* 思想；概念

　　　　develop 除了表有形事物的「發展」或「開發」外，
無形思想的構建培養也可以使用這個字。

十元硬幣上的是什麼花？

What's the flower on the 10-dollar coin?

That's the plum blossom.

It's the national flower of the R.O.C.

Its resilience symbolizes the Chinese character.

**

coin〔 kɔɪn 〕*n.* 硬幣　　plum〔 plʌm 〕*n.* 梅子；李子
blossom〔'blasəm 〕*n.*（樹的）花
plum blossom 梅花
resilience〔 rɪ'zɪlɪəns 〕*n.* 堅忍；適應力
symbolize〔'sɪmbḷˌaɪz 〕*v.* 象徵
character〔'kærɪktɚ〕*n.* 性格

【背景說明】

1. ***What's the flower on the 10-dollar coin?***

   coin〔kɔɪn〕*n.* 硬幣

   　　這句話的意思是「十元硬幣上的是什麼花？」也可
   說成：

   > What kind of flower is that on the 10-dollar
   > coin?（十元硬幣上的花是哪一種花？）
   > Do you know what the flower is on the
   > ten-dollar coin?
   > （你知道十元硬幣上的是什麼花嗎？）

2. ***That's the plum blossom.***

   plum〔plʌm〕*n.* 梅子；李子
   blossom〔'blɑsəm〕*n.* (樹的)花
   plum blossom 梅花

   　　這句話的意思是「那是梅花。」也可說成：It's
   the plum blossom.（它是梅花。）

   　　cherry tree（櫻花樹）開的花叫 cherry blossom
   （櫻花），apple tree（蘋果樹）開的花叫 apple
   blossom（蘋果花）。一般而言，樹所開的花的花名，
   要用樹名加 blossom。你可以說它們是 flower，但它
   們的名字一定是～ blossom。

3. *It's the national flower of the R.O.C.*
national flower 國花

　　這句話的意思是「它是中華民國的國花。」也可
說成：It's Taiwan's national flower.（它是台灣的
國花。）

4. *Its resilience symbolizes the Chinese character.*
resilience〔rɪ'zɪlɪəns〕*n.* 堅忍；適應力
symbolize〔'sɪmbḷ͵aɪz〕*v.* 象徵
character〔'kærɪktɚ〕*n.* 性格

　　這句話的意思是「它的堅忍象徵中國人的性格。」
也可説成：

　Its tough nature represents the Chinese
　　character.
　（它堅強的天性代表了中國人的性格。）
　It's ruggedness symbolizes how strong
　　the Chinese are.
　（它的堅忍不拔象徵中國人是多麼地堅強。）
　The resilient plum blossom represents the
　　rugged Chinese character.
　（梅花堅忍的特性代表了中國人堅強的性格。）

　tough〔tʌf〕*adj.* 堅強的；不屈的　nature〔'netʃɚ〕*n.* 本質
　ruggedness〔'rʌgɪd͵nɪs〕*n.* 強健
　resilient〔rɪ'zɪlɪənt〕*adj.* 適應力強的
　rugged〔'rʌgɪd〕*adj.* 堅強的

Question 30

誰是蔣介石？

Who was Chiang Kai-shek?

He was the second President of the R.O.C.

He led the Nationalists against the Japanese and Communist forces.

He was a firm and successful political leader, too.

** ───────────────

Nationalist (ˈnæʃənlˌɪst) *n.* 國家主義者 (在此指國民黨員)
lead (lid) *v.* 帶領　against (əˈgɛnst) *prep.* 對抗
Communist (ˈkɑmjuˌnɪst) *n.* 共產黨員　*adj.* 共產黨的
forces (forsɪz) *n. pl.* 軍隊　firm (fɝm) *adj.* 果斷的；強硬的
political leader 政治領袖

【背景說明】

1. *Who was Chiang Kai-shek?*

這句話的意思是「誰是蔣介石？」也可說成：

Can you please tell me about Chiang Kai-shek?
（可以請你告訴我關於蔣介石的事嗎？）

Would you mind telling me about Chiang
Kai-shek?（你介不介意告訴我關於蔣介石的事？）

【mind（maɪd）v. 介意】

2. *He was the second President of the R.O.C.*

這句話的意思是「他是中華民國的第二任總統。」
也可說成：General Chiang became the second
President of the R.O.C.（蔣將軍成了中華民國的第
二任總統。）【general（ˈdʒɛnərəl）n. 將軍】

3. *He led the Nationalists against the Japanese and Communist forces.*

lead（lid）v. 帶領
Nationalist（ˈnæʃənḷɪst）n. 國家主義者（在此指國民黨員）
against（əˈgɛnst）prep. 對抗
Communist（ˈkɑmjuˌnɪst）n. 共產黨員　adj. 共產黨的
forces（forsɪz）n. pl. 軍隊

這句話的意思是「他領導國民軍對抗日本和共產黨
的軍隊。」也可說成：

General Chiang's Nationalist army fought
the Japanese and then the Communists
for many years.

（蔣將軍的國民軍隊與日本及共產黨打了好幾年。）

The Nationalist army, led by Chiang Kai-shek
fought both the Japanese and the Communists.

（蔣介石所領導的國民軍隊與日本及共產黨打仗。）

【 fight〔faɪt〕*v.* 和～打仗　army〔'ɑrmɪ〕*n.* 軍隊 】

4. *He was a firm and successful political leader, too.*

firm〔fɝm〕*adj.* 果斷的；強硬的
political leader 政治領袖

這句話的意思是「他也是一個果決而且成功的政治
領袖。」也可說成：

He was a strict but successful political leader.

（他是一個嚴厲但成功的政治領袖。）

President Chiang ruled with strict authority.

（蔣總統以絕對的權威統治國家。）

Chiang had tight control but he accomplished
a lot.（蔣介石雖然治理國事嚴厲，但他有許多成就。）

strict〔strɪkt〕*adj.* 嚴厲的　authority〔ə'θɔrətɪ〕*n.* 權威
tight〔taɪt〕*adj.* 嚴厲的　accomplish〔ə'kɑmplɪʃ〕*v.* 完成

a lot 是名詞，作「許多」解。

台灣典型的日常三餐是什麼？

What are the three typical daily meals in Taiwan?

Breakfast is often soybean milk, steamed buns and rice soup.

Lunch and dinner are about the same.

Several meat and vegetable dishes with rice are the norm.

**

typical ('tɪpɪkḷ) *adj.* 典型的　　daily ('delɪ) *adj.* 日常的
meal (mil) *n.* 一餐　　soybean ('sɔɪ'bin) *n.* 大豆
soybean milk 豆漿　　steam (stim) *v.* 蒸
bun (bʌn) *n.* 小圓麵包　　*steamed bun* 饅頭
rice soup 粥；稀飯　　meat (mit) *n.* 肉　　dish (dɪʃ) *n.* 菜餚
rice (raɪs) *n.* 飯　　norm (nɔrm) *n.* 一般的標準

【背景説明】

1. ***What are the three typical daily meals in Taiwan?***
   typical (ˈtɪpɪkḷ) *adj.* 典型的　　daily (ˈdelɪ) *adj.* 日常的
   meal (mil) *n.* 一餐

   　　這句話的意思是「台灣典型的日常三餐是什麼？」
   也可説成：

   How do the foods for breakfast, lunch
   　　and dinner differ in Taiwan?
   （台灣早餐、午餐、晚餐的食物有什麼不同？）
   【differ (ˈdɪfɚ) *v.* 不同】

2. ***Breakfast is often soybean milk, steamed buns
   and rice soup.***
   soybean (ˈsɔɪˈbin) *n.* 大豆　　steam (stim) *v.* 蒸
   bun (bʌn) *n.* 小圓麵包　　***rice soup*** 粥；稀飯

   　　這句話的意思是「早餐通常是豆漿、饅頭和稀飯。」
   也可補充説：

   Taiwanese enjoy hot or cold soybean milk
   　　for a breakfast beverage.
   （台灣人喜歡將熱或冷的豆漿當作早餐的飲料。）
   Many younger people will often buy milk
   　　and rice balls at a convenience store.
   （許多比較年輕的人常會在便利商店買牛奶和飯糰。）
   【beverage (ˈbɛvrɪdʒ) *n.* 飲料　　***rice ball*** 飯糰】

3. *Lunch and dinner are about the same.*

about〔ə'baut〕*adv.* 大體上；差不多

這句話的意思是「午晚餐差不多一樣。」也可說
成：In Taiwan, lunches and dinners contain almost the
same things. (在台灣，午餐和晚餐包含的東西幾乎相同。)

【contain〔kən'ten〕*v.* 包含】

about 在這裡當副詞用，作表「大體上；差不多」
解，如：It's about time to leave. (差不多該離開了。)

4. *Several meat and vegetable dishes with rice are the norm.*

meat〔mit〕*n.* 肉　　dish〔dɪʃ〕*n.* 菜餚
rice〔raɪs〕*n.* 飯　　norm〔nɔrm〕*n.* 一般的標準

這句話的意思是「通常是幾道肉類和蔬菜搭配白
飯。」也可補充說：

Meat dishes of pork, fish, chicken and beef
are eaten at both meals.
(豬肉、魚肉、雞肉和牛肉等菜餚，會在這兩餐吃。)

Popular vegetables for both meals are
cauliflower, cabbage, gherkin, spinach
and loofah.
(這兩餐比較受歡迎的蔬菜有花椰菜、高麗菜、小黃
瓜、菠菜和絲瓜。)

pork〔pork〕*n.* 豬肉　　beef〔bif〕*n.* 牛肉
cauliflower〔'kɔlə,flauɚ〕*n.* 花椰菜
cabbage〔'kæbɪdʒ〕*n.* 高麗菜　　gherkin〔'gɝkɪn〕*n.* 小黃瓜
spinach〔'spɪnɪdʒ〕*n.* 菠菜　　loofah〔'lufə〕*n.* 絲瓜

台灣人如何祭拜神明？

How do Taiwanese worship their gods?

People offer sacrifices and burn incense and paper money.

Sacrifices usually include meats, fruits and beverages of all kinds.

People sometimes ask the gods to predict their future.

**

worship (ˈwɝʃəp) v. 祭拜　　offer (ˈɔfɚ) v. 供奉（祭品）
sacrifice (ˈsækrəˌfaɪs) n. 祭品　　burn (bɝn) v. 燃燒
incense (ɪnˈsɛns) n. 香　　*paper money* 紙錢
beverage (ˈbɛvrɪdʒ) n. 飲料
predict (prɪˈdɪkt) v. 預測；預言

【背景説明】

1. *How do Taiwanese worship their gods?*

   worship〔'wɝʃəp〕v. 祭拜

   　　　這句話的意思是「台灣人如何祭拜神明？」也可
   説成：

   In what ways do Taiwanese worship their gods?
   （台灣人用什麼方式祭拜他們的神明？）

   What worship rituals do Taiwanese practice?
   （台灣人實行什麼祭拜儀式？）

   【ritual〔'rɪtʃuəl〕n. 儀式　practice〔'præktɪs〕v. 實行】

2. *People offer sacrifices and burn incense and*
   paper money.

   offer〔'ɔfɚ〕v. 供奉（祭品）
   sacrifice〔'sækrə,faɪs〕n. 祭品
   incense〔ɪn'sɛns〕n. 香　　*paper money* 紙錢

   　　　這句話的意思是「人們供奉祭品並燒香和紙錢。」
   也可説成：

   Taiwanese like to offer food sacrifices to
   　the gods.（台灣人喜歡供奉食物祭品給神明。）
   People burn joss sticks, pray and then burn
   　spirit money.（人們燒香、祈禱，然後焚燒紙錢。）

   joss〔dʒɑs〕n.（中國的）神像　stick〔stɪk〕n.（細長的）棍棒
   pray〔pre〕v. 祈禱　*spirit money* 紙錢

incense 是泛指一般焚燒會產生香氣的香，通常
用以指祭祀時所焚的香；joss stick 也是指香，但它
是特別指中國人祭拜時所用的香。兩種說法都可以，
但口語上美國人較常用前者。紙錢也可以說成 spirit
money，但美國人通常會說 paper money。

3. **Sacrifices usually include meats, fruits and beverages of all kinds.**
   beverage〔ˈbɛvrɪdʒ〕*n.* 飲料

   這句話的意思是「祭品通常包括了肉、水果及各種
   飲料。」也可說成：

   Foods that are sacrificed include meats,
   fruits and beverages.
   （祭拜的食物通常包括了肉、水果及飲料。）

   Popular things to sacrifice are meats, fruits
   and beverages.
   （拿來祭拜的東西，常見的有肉、水果及飲料。）

4. **People sometimes ask the gods to predict their future.**
   predict〔prɪˈdɪkt〕*v.* 預測；預言

   這句話的意思是「人們有時會請求神明預言他們
   的未來。」也可說成：

   Worshippers ask the gods to predict their
   future.（祭拜者請求神明預言他們的未來。）

   People pray to the gods to tell them the future.
   （人們祈求神明告訴他們未來的事。）
   【worshipper〔ˈwɝʃəpɚ〕*n.* 祭拜者】

33　人們為什麼燒香和紙錢？

Why do people burn incense
and paper money?

People communicate with the gods and
their ancestors through the smoke.

People burn paper money for gods
and ancestors to use in heaven.

Burning incense is the most common
way to worship.

** ────────────────

incense (ɪn'sɛns) n. 香　**paper money** 紙錢
communicate (kə'mjunəˌket) v. 溝通
ancestor ('ænsɛstɚ) n. 祖先　through (θru) prep. 透過
heaven ('hɛvən) n. 天堂　worship ('wɝʃəp) v. 祭拜

【背景説明】

1. *Why do people burn incense and paper money?*
   incense〔ˋɪnˋsɛns〕*n.* 香　　*paper money* 紙錢

   　　這句話的意思是「人們為什麼燒香和紙錢？」也
   可説成：What is the reason for burning incense
   and paper money?（燒香和紙錢的理由是什麼？）

2. *People communicate with the gods and their ancestors through the smoke.*
   communicate〔kəˋmjunəˏket〕*v.* 溝通
   ancestor〔ˋænsɛstəˋ〕*n.* 祖先
   through〔θru〕*prep.* 透過；藉由

   　　這句話的意思是「人們藉由煙與神明及他們的祖先溝
   通。」也可説成：

   Many believe the smoke helps them to
   　　communicate with gods and ancestors.
   （許多人相信煙能幫助他們與神明及祖先溝通。）

   People use the smoke to talk to the gods
   　　and their ancestors.
   （人們利用煙與神明及他們祖先說話。）

   The smoke is believed to be a way to contact
   　　the gods and their ancestors.
   （煙被認為是一種與神明及他們祖先聯繫的方法。）

   【contact〔ˋkɑntækt〕*v.* 聯繫】

3. *People burn paper money for gods and ancestors to use in heaven.*

heaven ('hɛvən) *n.* 天堂

　　這句話的意思是「人們燒紙錢給神明和祖先在天堂使用。」也可說成：

The ritual of burning paper money is for gods and ancestors to use in the spirit world.

（燒紙錢的儀式是爲了給神明和祖先在靈界使用。）

Paper money is burned for gods and ancestors to use.

（紙錢是要燒給神明和祖先用的。）

【*spirit world* 幽靈的世界】

4. *Burning incense is the most common way to worship.*

common ('kɑmən) *adj.* 常見的
worship ('wɝʃəp) *v.* 祭拜

　　這句話的意思是「燒香是最常見的祭拜方式。」
也可說成：

Lighting up incense sticks is a popular way
　　to worship. （點香是一種普遍的祭拜方式。）

Burning incense is a typical way to pray.

（燒香是一種典型的的祈禱方式。）

light up 點燃　*incense stick* （一柱一柱的）香
typical ('tɪpɪkl̩) *adj.* 典型的

Question 34 台灣流行算命嗎？

Is fortune-telling popular in Taiwan?

Many Taiwanese have had their fortune told.

Most consult a fortune teller when they face an important decision.

There are many methods, like palm reading, divination and horoscope.

** ——————————————

fortune ('fɔrtʃən) *n.* 命運　***fortune-telling*** 算命
consult (kən'sʌlt) *v.* 請教　***fortune teller*** 算命師
decision (dɪ'sɪʒən) *n.* 決定　method ('mɛθəd) *n.* 方法
palm (pɑm) *n.* 手掌　divination (ˌdɪvə'neʃən) *n.* 占卜
horoscope ('hɔrəˌskop) *n.* 占星；星座

【背景說明】

1. ***Is fortune-telling popular in Taiwan?***

   fortune (ˈfɔrtʃən) *n.* 命運　***fortune-telling***　算命

   > 這句話的意思是「台灣流行算命嗎？」也可說成：

   Do Taiwanese like to have their fortune told?

   （台灣人喜歡算命嗎？）

   Are Taiwanese big fans of fortune-telling?

   （台灣人很熱衷算命嗎？）

   【*have one's fortune told* 請人算命　fan (fæn) *n.* 狂熱者；迷】

2. ***Many Taiwanese have had their fortune told.***

   > 這句話的意思是「許多台灣人算過命。」也可說成：

   Many Taiwanese have tried fortune-telling.

   （許多台灣人嘗試過算命。）

   A majority of Taiwanese have tried fortune-
   telling. (大多數的台灣人嘗試過算命。)

   【majority (məˈdʒɔrətɪ) *n.* 大多數】

3. ***Most consult a fortune teller when they face an
   important decision.***

   consult (kənˈsʌlt) *v.* 請教　***fortune teller***　算命師
   decision (dɪˈsɪʒən) *n.* 決定

   > 這句話的意思是「大多數的人在面臨重大決定時，
   > 會去請教算命師。」也可說成：

Most Taiwanese visit a fortune teller when
they have a tough choice to make.

（大部分的台灣人在很難做出選擇時，會去找算命師。）

Most Taiwanese use a fortune teller to make a
decision or solve a difficult problem.

（大部分台灣人會利用算命師來做出決定或解決難題。）

visit〔'vɪzɪt〕*v.* 拜訪　　tough〔tʌf〕*adj.* 困難的
decision〔dɪ'sɪʒən〕*n.* 決定　　solve〔sɑlv〕*v.* 解決

4. ***There are many methods, like palm reading,
divination and horoscope.***
method〔'mɛθəd〕*n.* 方法　　palm〔pɑm〕*n.* 手掌
divination〔,dɪvə'neʃən〕*n.* 占卜
horoscope〔'hɔrə,skop〕*n.* 占星；星座

　　這句話的意思是「有很多方法，像是看手相、占卜
和占星。」也可說成：

Fortune telling includes many methods in
Taiwan.（在台灣，算命包含了許多方法。）

There are a variety of ways to have your fortune
told in Taiwan.（在台灣，有許多方法能幫你算命。）

The art of fortune-telling comes in many forms
in Taiwan.（算命術在台灣有許多形式。）

【*a variety of* 各種的　　*come in* 有…（形式、顏色、大小等）】

　　art 不只是指藝術，專門的技術、技藝，以及為人處事
的技巧等，都是 art，如：art of cooking（烹飪術）、art of
healing（醫術）、art of communication（溝通技巧）等。

Question 35

什麼是陰曆？

What's the lunar calendar?

It was made according to the cycles of the moon.

It helps farmers determine the different times of the year.

Religious festivals are held on set days on the lunar calendar.

**

lunar ('lunɚ) *adj.* 月亮的　calendar ('kæləndɚ) *n.* 日曆
lunar calendar 陰曆；農曆　*according to* 根據
cycle ('saɪkḷ) *n.* 循環（期）　determine (dɪ'tɜmɪn) *v.* 決定
religious (rɪ'lɪdʒəs) *adj.* 宗教的
festival ('fɛstəvḷ) *n.* 慶典；節日
hold (hold) *v.* 舉行　set (sɛt) *adj.* 固定的

【背景説明】

1. ***What's the lunar calendar?***

   lunar (ˈlunɚ) *adj.* 月亮的　　calendar (ˈkæləndɚ) *n.* 日曆
   lunar calendar 陰曆；農曆（陽曆則是 solar calendar。）

   這句話的意思是「什麼是陰曆？」也可説成：

   What does the term "lunar calendar" mean?
   （陰曆這個名詞是什麼意思？）
   What is a lunar calendar? (什麼是陰曆？)

2. ***It was made according to the cycles of the moon.***

   according to 根據　　cycle (ˈsaɪkḷ) *n.* 循環（期）

   這句話的意思是「它是根據月亮的週期制定的。」
   也可説成：

   It is determined by the period between full
   moons. (它是由滿月與滿月之間的那段期間所決定。)
   The lunar calendar was established according
   to the cycles of the moon.
   （陰曆的制定是根據月亮的週期。）

   【determine (dɪˈtɜmɪn) *v.* 決定】

   according to 當介系詞使用，表示「根據」，後面
   可接人、文件、計劃、原理等。當後面接人時，表示
   根據某人所説的話，但不可使用 *according to me*（誤），
   若想表達自己的意見，可用 in my opinion（我認為…）。

3. *It helps farmers determine the different times of the year.*

determine〔dɪ'tɝmɪn〕v. 決定

這句話的意思是「它幫助農民決定一年之中不同的
時期。」也可以說：

The lunar calendar helps farmers make
crop decisions.

（陰曆幫助農民決定農作物的播種與收割。）

It gives farmers information on times and
seasons. (它提供農民時期和季節的資訊。)

【crop〔krɑp〕n. 農作物】

4. *Religious festivals are held on set days on the lunar*
calendar.

religious〔rɪ'lɪdʒəs〕adj. 宗教的
festival〔'fɛstəvl〕n. 慶典；節日
hold〔hold〕v. 舉行　　set〔sɛt〕adj. 固定的

這句話的意思是「宗敎性的慶典會在陰曆的固定日
子舉行。」也可說成：

Religious ceremonies are held on specific
dates of the lunar calendar.

（宗敎儀式在陰曆特定的日子舉行。）

Religious activities occur on set dates
according to the lunar calendar.

（宗敎活動根據陰曆在固定的日期舉行。）

ceremony〔'sɛrə,monɪ〕n. 儀式　specific〔spɪ'sɪfɪk〕adj. 特定的
activity〔æk'tɪvətɪ〕n. 活動　occur〔ə'kɝ〕v. 發生

36 台灣的婚禮是什麼樣子？

What's a wedding like in Taiwan?

It's more like a banquet than a ceremony.

The newlyweds feast with family and friends.

Guests give red envelopes of cash as gifts.

**

wedding (ˈwɛdɪŋ) *n.* 婚禮　banquet (ˈbæŋkwɪt) *n.* 宴會
ceremony (ˈsɛrə,monɪ) *n.* 典禮
newlyweds (ˈnjulɪ,wɛds) *n. pl.* 新婚夫婦
feast (fist) *v.* 大吃；飽餐；設宴款待
red envelope 紅包　cash (kæʃ) *n.* 現金
guest (gɛst) *n.* 客人

【背景説明】

1. **What's a wedding like in Taiwan?**
   wedding (ˈwɛdɪŋ) *n.* 婚禮

   　　這句話的意思是「台灣的婚禮是什麼樣子？」也可
   說成：Can you describe a typical Taiwanese wedding?
   （你可以描述一下典型的台灣婚禮嗎？）
   【describe (dɪˈskraɪb) *v.* 描述　typical (ˈtɪpɪkl̩) *adj.* 典型的】

2. **It's more like a banquet than a ceremony.**
   banquet (ˈbæŋkwɪt) *n.* 宴會
   ceremony (ˈsɛrə͵monɪ) *n.* 典禮

   　　這句話的意思是「它比較像宴會，不像典禮。」
   也可説成：

   　It's more like a feast than a ritual.
   　（它比較像宴會，不像儀式。）
   　Taiwanese weddings are basically a big, party-like
   　　meal. (台灣的婚禮基本上是個大型的聚會餐宴。)
   　feast (fist) *n.* 盛宴　ritual (ˈrɪtʃʊəl) *n.* 儀式
   　basically (ˈbesɪkəlɪ) *adv.* 本質上；基本上

3. **The newlyweds feast with family and friends.**
   newlyweds (ˈnjulɪ͵wɛdz) *n. pl.* 新婚夫婦
   feast (fist) *v.* 大吃；飽餐；設宴款待

   　　這句話的意思是「新婚夫婦會和家人及朋友一起飽
   餐一頓。」也可説成：

The newly married couple host a huge meal
for everyone.

（新婚夫婦會爲大家舉行一個大型餐會。）

The bride and groom celebrate a big meal
with family and friends.

（新娘和新郎爲家人和朋友舉行一個大型餐會。）

The newlyweds have a multi-course meal
with loved ones and friends.

（新婚夫婦和親人及朋友一起吃一頓大餐。）

married (ˈmærɪd) *adj.* 已婚的　couple (ˈkʌpl̩) *n.* 夫婦
host (host) *v.* 當宴會主人　bride (braɪd) *n.* 新娘
groom (grum) *n.* 新郎　celebrate (ˈsɛlə,bret) *v.* 舉行；慶祝
multi- (,mʌltɪ) 多…（複合用詞）　course (kors) *n.* 一道(菜)
loved ones 親人

4. *Guests give red envelopes of cash as gifts.*

guest (gɛst) *n.* 客人　envelope (ˈɛnvə,lop) *n.* 信封
red envelope 紅包　cash (kæʃ) *n.* 現金

這句話的意思是「客人給現金紅包當作禮物。」
也可說成：

Wedding guests give money in red envelopes
as gifts. (婚禮賓客會給裝了錢的紅包當作禮物。)

Wedding attendees give cash in "hong baos"
as gifts.

（婚禮出席者會給裝了現金的紅包當作禮物。）

【attendee (ə,tɛnˈdi) *n.* 出席者】

Question 37　台灣的葬禮是什麼樣子？

What's a funeral like in Taiwan?

Funerals are complicated and may last many days or weeks.

Family members wear white ribbons or white robes to mourn.

They burn paper objects for the dead to use in the spirit world.

** ————————————————————

funeral ('fjunərəl) *n.* 葬禮
complicated ('kɑmplə,ketɪd) *adj.* 複雜的
last (læst) *v.* 持續　　ribbon ('rɪbən) *n.* 緞帶
robe (rob) *n.* 長袍　　mourn (morn) *v.* 服喪
object ('ɑbdʒɪkt) *n.* 物品
the dead 死者 (= *dead people*)　　*spirit world* 幽靈世界

【背景説明】

1. ***What's a funeral like in Taiwan?***
   funeral (ˈfjunərəl) *n.* 葬禮

   　　這句話的意思是「台灣的葬禮是什麼樣子？」也可説成：

   How are funerals in Taiwan?
   （台灣的葬禮是怎麼樣？）
   Can you explain a typical Taiwanese funeral?
   （你可以說明典型的台灣葬禮嗎？）

   explain (ɪkˈsplen) *v.* 解釋；說明
   typical (ˈtɪpɪkḷ) *adj.* 典型的

2. ***Funerals are complicated and may last many days
   or weeks.***
   complicated (ˈkɑmpləˌketɪd) *adj.* 複雜的
   last (læst) *v.* 持續

   　　這句話的意思是「葬禮很複雜，而且可能會持續許
   多天或幾個禮拜。」也可説成：

   Funerals may last a long time and are not
   　　simple ceremonies.
   （葬禮可能持續一段很長的時間，而且不是簡單的儀式。）
   A Taiwanese funeral may last weeks and it's
   　　not a simple matter.
   （台灣的葬禮可能會持續幾個禮拜，不是一件簡單的事。）

   ceremony (ˈsɛrəˌmonɪ) *n.* 典禮；儀式
   matter (ˈmætə) *n.* 事情

3. ***Family members wear white ribbons or white robes to mourn.***

member〔'mɛmbɚ〕*n.* 成員　　ribbon〔'rɪbən〕*n.* 緞帶
robe〔rob〕*n.* 長袍　　mourn〔morn〕*v.* 服喪

　　這句話的意思是「家庭成員會披上白色布條或穿白袍服喪。」也可以說：

　　The family members wear white to honor
　　　the deceased.

　　（家庭成員會穿白色的衣服表示對已故者的敬意。）

　　Relatives of the deceased wear white robes
　　　during the mourning period.

　　（死者家屬會在服喪期間穿白袍。）

deceased〔dɪ'sist〕*adj.* 死亡的　***the deceased*** 死者
honor〔'ɑnɚ〕*v.* 向～表示敬意　relative〔'rɛlətɪv〕*n.* 親戚
period〔'pɪrɪəd〕*n.* 期間

4. ***They burn paper objects for the dead to use in the spirit world.***

object〔'ɑbdʒɪkt〕*n.* 物品　　***spirit world*** 幽靈世界

　　這句話的意思是「他們燒紙做的物品給死者在幽靈世界使用。」也可說成：Paper objects are burned for use in the afterlife.（燒紙做的東西是爲了要在死後的世界使用。）

【afterlife〔'æftɚ͵laɪf〕*n.* 死後的生活】

38 有任何關於鬼的風俗嗎？

Are there any customs involving ghosts?

Spirit marriage is popular in Taiwan.

It is practiced to appease the souls of single young girls who have died.

The spirit wife will boost her living husband's career.

**

involve〔ɪn'vɑlv〕v. 與～有關　ghost〔gost〕n. 鬼
spirit marriage 冥婚　practice〔'præktɪs〕v. 實行
appease〔ə'piz〕v. 撫慰　soul〔sol〕n. 亡靈
single〔'sɪŋgl̩〕adj. 單身的　***spirit wife*** 冥妻
boost〔bust〕v. 推動；增強　living〔'lɪvɪŋ〕adj. 活的
career〔kə'rɪr〕n. 事業

【背景說明】

1. ***Are there any customs involving ghosts?***

   involve〔ɪn'vɑlv〕 v. 與…有關　　ghost〔gost〕 n. 鬼

   這句話的意思是「有任何關於鬼的風俗嗎？」也
   可說成：

   Does Taiwan have any unusual customs
   involving ghosts?

   （台灣有任何的關於鬼的不尋常風俗嗎？）

   Are there any strange rituals or customs involving
   spirits?（有任何關於幽靈的奇怪風俗嗎？）

   Can you tell me if Taiwan has any weird or spooky
   customs?

   （你能不能告訴我台灣是否有任何奇異或鬼的風俗嗎？）

   unusual〔ʌn'juʒuəl〕 adj. 不尋常的　　spirit〔'spɪrɪt〕 n. 幽靈
   weird〔wɪrd〕 adj. 怪異的　　spooky〔'spukɪ〕 adj. 有鬼的

2. ***Spirit marriage is popular in Taiwan.***

   spirit marriage 冥婚

   這句話的意思是「冥婚在台灣很普遍。」也可說成：

   The custom of spirit marriage is not uncommon
   in Taiwan.（冥婚的風俗在台灣並不稀奇。）

   Many Taiwanese accept and believe in spirit
   marriages.（許多台灣人接受並相信冥婚是好的。）

   uncommon〔ʌn'kɑmən〕 adj. 罕見的
   accept〔ək'sɛpt〕 v. 接受　　***believe in*** 相信…是好的

3. *It is practiced to appease the souls of single young*
   girls who have died.

appease〔ə'piz〕*v.* 撫慰　　soul〔sol〕*n.* 亡靈

single〔'sɪŋgl〕*adj.* 單身的

　　　這句話的意思是「實行冥婚是為了撫慰已故的年
輕單身女子的亡魂。」也可說成：

Taiwanese practice use this custom to pacify the

lonely soul of a single woman who has died.

（ 台灣人實行這風俗來撫慰已故單身女子寂寞的靈魂。）

practice〔'præktɪs〕*v.* 實行　　pacify〔'pæsə,faɪ〕*v.* 撫慰

lonely〔'lonlɪ〕*adj.* 寂寞的

4. *The spirit wife will boost her living husband's career.*

spirit wife 冥妻　　boost〔bust〕*v.* 推動；增強

living〔'lɪvɪŋ〕*adj.* 活的　　career〔kə'rɪr〕*n.* 事業

　　　這句話的意思是「冥妻會推動他陽世丈夫的事業。」
也可以說：

People believe that a spirit wife will benefit

the man's career.

（ 人們相信冥妻會對男人的事業有幫助。）

Many think the man's fortunes will improve

if he has a spirit wife.

（ 許多人認為，如果男人有個冥妻，他的運氣會更好。）

【benefit〔'bɛnəfɪt〕*v.* 使獲益　　fortune〔'fɔrtʃən〕*n.* 運氣】

有任何關於吃的禁忌嗎？

Are there any taboos concerning eating?

Yes, never stick chopsticks vertically into food.

This is only done at funerals.

This is a common blunder committed by foreigners.

**

taboo〔tə'bu〕*n.* 禁忌　concerning〔kən'sɜnɪŋ〕*prep.* 關於
stick〔stɪk〕*v.* 刺；插入　chopsticks〔'tʃɑp͵stɪks〕*n. pl.* 筷子
vertically〔'vɜtɪkḷɪ〕*adv.* 垂直地
funeral〔'fjunərəl〕*n.* 葬禮　blunder〔'blʌndə〕*n.* 錯誤
commit〔kə'mɪt〕*v.* 犯（錯）；犯（罪）
foreigner〔'fɔrɪnə〕*n.* 外國人

【背景說明】

1. *Are there any taboos concerning eating?*

   taboo〔təˈbu〕*n.* 禁忌
   concerning〔kənˈsɜnɪŋ〕*prep.* 與…有關

   　　這句話的意思是「有任何關於吃的禁忌嗎？」也可
   說成：

   Are there any taboos or special table manners
   　concerning eating?
   （有任何關於吃的禁忌或特別的餐桌禮儀嗎？）

   Is there any eating custom that is considered
   　unlucky or impolite?
   （有任何吃的習俗被認為是不吉利或不禮貌的嗎？）

   table manners 餐桌禮儀　　impolite〔ˌɪmpəˈlaɪt〕*adj.* 無禮的

2. *Yes, never stick chopsticks vertically into food.*

   stick〔stɪk〕*v.* 刺；插入　　chopsticks〔ˈtʃɑpˌstɪks〕*n. pl.* 筷子
   vertically〔ˈvɜtɪklɪ〕*adv.* 垂直地

   　　這句話的意思是「有，絕對不能把筷子垂直地插在
   食物上。」也可說成：

   One major faux pas is to put your chopsticks
   　straight up into your food.
   （把筷子垂直插在你的食物上，是個非常失禮的行為。）

   Yes, you can't put chopsticks vertically into
   　　food.（有，你不可以把筷子垂直地插在食物上。）

   【faux pas〔ˌfoˈpɑ〕*n.* 失禮　　straight〔stret〕*adv.* 直立地】

3. ***This is only done at funerals.***

funeral (ˈfjunərəl) *n.* 葬禮

這句話的意思是「只有在葬禮上才會這麼做。」

也可說成：

Sticking chopsticks vertically into a bowl
of rice is a funeral ritual.

（把筷子垂直地插在一碗飯上，是一種葬禮的儀式。）

This practice is reserved only for funerals,
while offering food to the deceased.

（這個做法是忌諱的，只有在葬禮對死者祭上食物
時才會做。）

bowl (bol) *n.* 碗　　rice (raɪs) *n.* 飯
reserved (rɪˈzɜvd) *adj.* 忌諱的　　offer (ˈɔfɚ) *v.* 供奉（祭品）
deceased (dɪˈsist) *adj.* 死亡的（the ～ 死者）

4. ***This is a common blunder committed by foreigners.***

blunder (ˈblʌndɚ) *n.* 錯誤
commit (kəˈmɪt) *v.* 犯（錯）
foreigner (ˈfɔrɪnɚ) *n.* 外國人

這句話的意思是「這是外國人一般會犯的錯誤。」

也可說成：Many foreign visitors make this
mistake.（許多外國觀光客會犯這種錯。）

40 台灣人信仰什麼宗教？

What religions do Taiwanese follow?

Most people believe in folk religions.

Folk religions mix Confucianism, Taoism and Buddhism.

There are also Buddhists, Taoists, Christians, Muslims, etc.

**

religion (rɪ'lɪdʒən) *n.* 宗教
follow ('falo) *v.* 採用；支持；追隨
folk (fok) *adj.* 民間的   mix (mɪks) *v.* 混合
Confucianism (kən'fjuʃənɪzm) *n.* 儒家思想
Taoism ('tauɪzəm) *n.* 道教   Buddhism ('budɪzm) *n.* 佛教
Buddhist ('budɪst) *n.* 佛教徒   Taoist ('tauɪst) *n.* 道教徒
Christian ('krɪstʃən) *n.* 基督徒
Muslim ('mʌzləm) *n.* 回教徒

【背景說明】

1. ***What religions do Taiwanese follow?***

religion (rɪˈlɪdʒən) *n.* 宗教

follow (ˈfɑlo) *v.* 採用；支持；追隨

　　這句話的意思是「台灣人信仰什麼宗教？」也可說成：What are the popular religions in Taiwan?
（什麼是台灣普遍的宗教？）

2. ***Most people believe in folk religions.***

folk (fok) *adj.* 民間的　　***believe in*** 信仰

　　這句話的意思是「大部分的人信仰民間宗教。」也可說成：

Most Taiwanese follow the religious customs
　　of the common people.
（大部分台灣人會遵照一般人民的宗教風俗。）

Most people in Taiwan believe in a mix
　　of religious customs.
（大部分台灣人信奉混合的宗教風俗。）

【mix (mɪks) *n.* 混合（物）】

　　believe 是指「相信某人所說的話或者是某件事」，而 believe in 則表示：(1)相信…的存在，如：I believe in God. (我相信上帝的存在。)；(2)相信某個想法或政策是好的，如：He believes in marriage. (他相信婚姻是有好處的。)；(3)對某人的想法或做法有信心，如：I believe in my father. (我對我爸有信心。)

3. *Folk religions mix Confucianism, Taoism and Buddhism*.

mix〔mɪks〕*v.* 混合
Confucianism〔kənˈfjuʃənɪzm̩〕*n.* 儒家思想
Taoism〔ˈtauɪzəm〕*n.* 道教
Buddhism〔ˈbudɪzəm〕*n.* 佛教

　　這句話的意思是「民間信仰混合了儒教、道教和佛教。」也可說成：Taiwanese folk religions combine bits of Confucianism, Taoism and Buddhism.
（台灣民間信仰結合了少許的儒教、道教和佛教。）

【combine〔kəmˈbaɪn〕*v.* 結合　*bits of* 少許的】

4. *There are also Buddhists, Taoists, Christians, Muslims, etc*.

Buddhist〔ˈbudɪst〕*n.* 佛教徒
Taoist〔ˈtauɪst〕*n.* 道教徒
Christian〔ˈkrɪstʃən〕*n.* 基督徒
Muslim〔ˈmʌzləm〕*n.* 回教徒
etc.〔ɛtˈsɛtərə〕等等（拉丁文 et cetera 的簡寫）

　　這句話的意思是「也有佛教徒、道教徒、基督徒、回教徒等等。」也可說成：Taiwanese also follow religions like Buddhism, Taoism, Christianity and Islam.（台灣人也信仰像佛教、道教、基督教和回教等宗教。）

【Islam〔ˈɪsləm〕*n.* 伊斯蘭教；回教】

　　使用 etc. 時，它的前面要加逗點，前面提及的名詞需有兩個以上，且名詞間不可用 and 連接。

台灣一般的問候語是什麼？

What's a common greeting in Taiwan?

You can say, "Ni hao"(hello) or "Ni hao ma" (How are you?).

You can also ask, "Have you eaten?" (Ni chr gwo le ma?)

This is a special way of showing concern when greeting someone.

** ————————————————————

common ('kɑmən) *adj.* 常見的；一般的
greeting ('gritɪŋ) *n.* 問候　　show (ʃo) *v.* 表現
concern (kən'sɝn) *n.* 關心
greet (grit) *v.* 和～打招呼

【背景說明】

1. ***What's a common greeting in Taiwan?***

   common (ˈkɑmən) *adj.* 常見的；一般的

   greeting (ˈgritɪŋ) *n.* 問候

   > 這句話的意思是「台灣一般的問候語是什麼？」
   >
   > 也可以說：

   > How do people greet each other in Taiwan?
   > （在台灣，人們如何互相打招呼？）
   > What should I say while greeting someone
   > in Taiwan?
   > （在台灣和別人打招呼時我應該說什麼？）

2. ***You can say*, "*Ni hao*"(*hello*) *or* "*Ni hao ma*"**
   (*How are you?*).

   > 這句話的意思是「你可以說『你好』或『你好
   > 嗎？』。」也可說成：

   > Learn to say, "Ni Hao" and "Ni hao ma",
   > which mean hello and how are you.
   > （學習說"Ni Hao"和"Ni hao ma"，意思是
   > 你好和你好嗎。）
   > Be able to say hello and how are you in
   > Chinese. （要會說中文的你好和你好嗎。）

   > 美國人打招呼時，一般都說 How are you?（你
   > 好嗎？）；若與初次見面的人打招呼，則用 How do
   > you do?（你好嗎？）是屬於比較鄭重的用法。

3. ***You can also ask***, **"*Have you eaten?*"** (*Ni chr gwo le ma?*)

　　這句話的意思是「你也可以說『你吃飽了嗎？』。」
也可以說：

Saying "have you eaten" (Ni chr gwo le ma?)
　　is also popular.

（說「你吃飽了嗎？」也是很普遍。）

Asking someone if they have eaten (Ni chr gwo
le ma?) is a common greeting in Taiwan.

（問某人「吃飽了嗎？」是一般的台灣問候語。）

4. ***This is a special way of showing concern when greeting someone.***

show〔ʃo〕v. 表現　　concern〔kən'sɝn〕n. 關心

　　這句話的意思是「這是一種問候別人時表現關心的
特別方式。」也可說成：

It's a caring way to greet someone.

（這是一種關心方式的問候。）

This greeting is unique to Chinese and it
　　shows a friendly manner.

（這種問候語是中國人獨有的，它能表現出友善的態度。）

caring〔'kɛrɪŋ〕adj. 關心的　　***be unique to*** 是…所特有的
friendly〔'frɛndlɪ〕adj. 友善的　　manner〔'mænɚ〕n. 態度

Question 42　台灣人如何對待外國人？

How do Taiwanese treat foreigners?

Taiwanese are friendly and polite.

They like and welcome foreign guests.

Taiwanese are famous for being
hospitable.

**

treat (trit) *v.* 對待　foreigner (ˈfɔrɪnɚ) *n.* 外國人
friendly (ˈfrɛndlɪ) *adj.* 友善的
polite (pəˈlaɪt) *adj.* 有禮貌的
foreign (ˈfɔrɪn) *adj.* 外國的　guest (gɛst) *n.* 客人
famous (ˈfeməs) *adj.* 有名的
hospitable (ˈhɑspɪtəbl̩) *adj.* 好客的

【背景説明】

1. ### How do Taiwanese treat foreigners?

    treat〔trit〕*v.* 對待　　foreigner〔'fɔrɪnɚ〕*n.* 外國人

    這句話的意思是「台灣人如何對待外國人？」也可
    説成：

    Are Taiwanese nice to foreigners?

    （台灣人對外國人親切嗎？）

    Do Taiwanese sincerely welcome foreigners
    in Taiwan?

    （在台灣，台灣人會衷心地歡迎外國人嗎？）

    【*be nice to* 對…親切　　sincerely〔sɪn'sɪrlɪ〕*adv.* 衷心地】

2. ### Taiwanese are friendly and polite.

    friendly〔'frɛndlɪ〕*adj.* 友善的
    polite〔pə'laɪt〕*adj.* 有禮貌的

    這句話的意思是「台灣人幾乎都很友善，而且有
    禮貌。」也可説成：

    Taiwanese are courteous and kind.

    （台灣人很有禮貌而且親切。）

    Most Taiwanese are friendly to foreigners.

    （大部分的台灣人都對外國人很友善。）

    【courteous〔'kɜtɪəs〕*adj.* 有禮貌的】

3. **They like and welcome foreign guests**.

foreign ('fɔrɪn) adj. 外國的　　guest (gɛst) n. 客人

這句話的意思是「他們喜歡且歡迎外國客人。」

也可說成：

Taiwanese like foreigners and enjoy their
company.
（台灣人喜歡外國人，也喜歡跟他們在一起。）

In Taiwan, people are very hospitable towards
foreigners. (台灣人對外國人非常好客。）

company ('kʌmpənɪ) n. 陪伴
towards ('tordz) prep. 對於… (= toward)

4. **Taiwanese are famous for being hospitable**.

famous ('feməs) adj. 有名的
hospitable ('hɑspɪtəbl̩) adj. 好客的

這句話的意思是「台灣人的好客是很有名的。」

也可說成：

Taiwanese have a reputation for being
hospitable. (台灣人擁有好客的名聲。）

All foreigners know that Taiwanese are the
friendliest people.
（所有的外國人都知道，台灣人是最友善的。）

The people of Taiwan are noted for treating
foreigners great. (台灣人以對待外國人很好而聞名。）

reputation (ˌrɛpjə'teʃən) n. 名聲
noted ('notɪd) adj. 有名的　　great (gret) adv. 很好地

誰是孔子？

Who was Confucius?

He was China's greatest philosopher and teacher.

He has influenced Chinese thought and behavior deeply.

Confucianism affects politics, ethics, education and culture.

**

Confucius〔kən'fjuʃəs〕*n.* 孔子
philosopher〔fə'lɑsəfɚ〕*n.* 哲學家
influence〔'ɪnfluəns〕*v.* 影響 (= *affect*)
behavior〔bɪ'hevjɚ〕*n.* 行爲
Confucianism〔kən'fjuʃənɪzm̩〕*n.* 儒家思想
politics〔'pɑlə,tɪks〕*n.* 政治   ethics〔'ɛθɪks〕*n.* 倫理

【背景説明】

1. ***Who was Confucius?***

   Confucius〔kən'fjuʃəs〕*n.* 孔子

   這句話的意思是「誰是孔子？」也可説成：

   Was Confucius a real person or a myth?
   （孔子是眞有其人還是一個神話人物？）

   What did Confucius do to be such a big part
   of Chinese history?
   （孔子做了什麼，使他成爲中國歷史上如此重要的
   一部分？）【myth〔mɪθ〕*n.* 神話（人物）】

2. ***He was China's greatest philosopher and teacher.***

   philosopher〔fə'lɑsəfɚ〕*n.* 哲學家

   這句話的意思是「他是中國最偉大的哲學家和老
   師。」也可説成：

   Confucius was China's most influential educator.
   （孔子是中國最具影響力的教育家。）

   His ideas and philosophy permeate Chinese
   culture.（他的思想和哲學滲入中國文化。）

   In the realm of education and philosophy,
   Confucius has no equals.
   （在教育和哲學的領域，無人可與孔子匹敵。）

   influential〔ˌɪnflʊ'ɛnʃəl〕*adj.* 有影響力的
   educator〔'ɛdʒʊˌketɚ〕*n.* 敎育家
   philosophy〔fə'lɑsəfɪ〕*n.* 哲學　permeate〔'pɝmɪˌet〕*v.* 滲入
   realm〔rɛlm〕*n.* 領域　　equal〔'ikwəl〕*n.* 相匹敵的人

3. *He has influenced Chinese thought and behavior deeply*.

influence (ˈɪnflʊəns) *v.* 影響

behavior (bɪˈhevjɚ) *n.* 行為　　deeply (ˈdiplɪ) *adv.* 深深地

這句話的意思是「他深深地影響了中國人的思想和
行為。」也可說成：

Confucius has left a deep impression on
Chinese culture.

（孔子對中國文化留下深刻的影響。）

No one person has influenced China more
than Confucius.

（孔子對中國的影響沒有人比得上。）

【impression (ɪmˈprɛʃən) *n.* 影響】

4. *Confucianism affects politics, ethics, education
and culture*.

Confucianism (kənˈfjuʃənɪzm̩) *n.* 儒家思想

affect (əˈfɛkt) *v.* 影響　　politics (ˈpɑləˌtɪks) *n.* 政治

ethics (ˈɛθɪks) *n.* 倫理

這句話的意思是「儒家思想影響了政治、倫理、教
育和文化。」也可說成：Confucianism influences
almost all realms of Chinese society. （儒家思想幾
乎影響了中國社會的所有領域。）

什麼是孝順？

What is filial piety?

This is the concept of respect for parents.

Children must try to obey their parents' wishes.

Children are responsible for elderly parents.

** ─────────────

filial ('fɪlɪəl) *adj.* 子女的

piety ('paɪətɪ) *n.* 虔敬；孝順　　concept ('kɑnsɛpt) *n.* 觀念

respect (rɪ'spɛkt) *n.* 尊敬　　obey (ə'be) *v.* 服從

wish (wɪʃ) *n.* 願望；要求

responsible (rɪ'spɑnsəbḷ) *adj.* 對⋯有責任的

elderly ('ɛldɚlɪ) *adj.* 年長的

【背景説明】

1. *What is filial piety?*

    filial (ˈfɪlɪəl) *adj.* 子女的　　piety (ˈpaɪətɪ) *n.* 虔敬；孝順
    filial piety 孝順

    這句話的意思是「什麼是孝順？」也可説成：

    What does the term filial piety mean?
    （孝順這個名詞是什麼意思？）
    What is the concept of filial piety all about?
    （孝順的概念是什麼？）

    What is(are) A all about? (A 是關於什麼？) A 必須
    是無形的事情、概念等，而非有形的物體。這是美國人常
    用的口語問句，加在句尾的 all about 有一種希望對整件
    事情有概略性了解的意味。

2. *This is the concept of respect for parents.*

    concept (ˈkɑnsɛpt) *n.* 觀念　　respect (rɪˈspɛkt) *n.* 尊敬

    這句話的意思是「這是一種尊敬父母的觀念。」
    也可説成：

    This is the custom of obeying and honoring
        your parents.
    （這是一種順從和尊敬父母的習俗。）
    This idea means that children must be devoted
        to their parents.
    （這個觀念的意思是孩子必須摯愛父母。）
    【honor (ˈɑnɚ) *v.* 尊敬　　devoted (dɪˈvotɪd) *adj.* 摯愛的】

3. *Children must try to obey their parents' wishes.*

obey〔ə'be〕v. 服從　　wish〔wɪʃ〕n. 願望；要求

這句話的意思是「孩子必須試著去遵從父母的要求。」也可以說：

Chinese children must be obedient to their parents. (中國小孩必須順從他們的父母。)

The parents' wishes almost always must be obeyed. (父母的要求幾乎總是必須服從。)

【obedient〔ə'bidɪənt〕adj. 服從的】

4. *Children are responsible for elderly parents.*

responsible〔rɪ'spɑnsəbḷ〕adj. 對…有責任的

elderly〔'ɛldəlɪ〕adj. 年長的

這句話的意思是「孩子對年長的父母有責任。」也可說成：

In Chinese culture, elderly parents are the kids' responsibility.

(在中國文化中，年長的父母是孩子的責任。)

It's very important that children take responsibility for elderly parents.

(孩子負起對年老父母的責任是很重要的。)

【responsibility〔rɪ,spɑnsə'bɪlətɪ〕n. 責任】

Question 45

中醫是關於些什麼？

What is Chinese medicine all about?

It treats and maintains balance in "the whole body."

It prevents illness with combinations of natural herbs.

Chinese medicine includes massage, acupuncture, skin scraping, etc.

**

maintain (men'ten) v. 維持　balance ('bæləns) n. 平衡
prevent (prɪ'vɛnt) v. 預防
combination (ˌkɑmbə'neʃən) n. 搭配
herb (hɜb) n. 藥草　massage (mə'sɑʒ) n. 推拿；按摩
acupuncture ('ækjuˌpʌŋktʃɚ) n. 針灸
scraping ('skrepɪŋ) n. 刮；擦　*etc.*(ɛt'sɛtərə)等等

【背景説明】

1. ***What is Chinese medicine all about?***

   medicine (ˈmɛdəsṇ) *n.* 醫學；藥

   這句話的意思是「中醫是關於些什麼？」也可説成：

   What is the basic philosophy behind Chinese
   medicine? (中醫背後的基本原理是什麼？)

   Why is Chinese medicine still so popular in our
   modern era? (爲什麼在現代中醫仍然這麼流行？)

   basic (ˈbesɪk) *adj.* 基本的
   philosophy (fəˈlɑsəfɪ) *n.* 哲理；原理　　era (ˈɪrə) *n.* 時代

2. ***It treats and maintains balance in "the whole body."***

   treat (trit) *v.* 治療　　maintain (menˈten) *v.* 維持
   balance (ˈbæləns) *n.* 平衡

   這句話的意思是「它治療並維持整個身體的平衡。」
   也可説成：

   Chinese medicine is based on a holistic
   approach. (中醫是以整體的觀點爲根據。)

   The goal of Chinese medicine is to maintain
   balance in the body.
   (中醫的目的是維持身體的平衡。)

   holistic (hoˈlɪstɪk) *adj.* 全部的；整體的
   be based on 以…爲根據；基於…
   approach (əˈprotʃ) *n.* 觀點　　goal (gol) *n.* 目的

3. *It prevents illness with combinations of natural herbs.*
prevent〔prɪˈvɛnt〕*v.* 預防
combination〔ˌkɑmbəˈneʃən〕*n.* 搭配；結合
herb〔hɝb〕*n.* 藥草

　　這句話的意思是「它用搭配的天然藥草來預防疾病。」
也可以說成：

Chinese medicine treats and prevents disease
by using traditional herbs.
（中醫藉著使用傳統藥草來治療並預防疾病。）
It uses natural herbs to fight disease.
（它使用天然的藥草來對抗疾病。）

【traditional〔trəˈdɪʃən!〕*adj.* 傳統的　fight〔faɪt〕*v.* 對抗】

4. *Chinese medicine includes massage, acupuncture,*
skin scraping, etc.
acupuncture〔ˈækjʊˌpʌŋktʃɚ〕*n.* 針灸
skin〔skɪn〕*n.* 皮膚　scraping〔ˈskrepɪŋ〕*n.* 刮；擦

　　這句話的意思是「中醫包括了推拿、針灸和刮痧
等等。」也可說成：

There are many facets to Chinese medicine.
（中醫有很多方面。）
Chinese medicine includes many different
treatments such as massage, acupuncture
and skin scraping.
（中醫包括了許多不同的治療法，像是推拿、針灸和刮痧。）

facet〔ˈfæsɪt〕*n.*（事物的）面　treatment〔ˈtritmənt〕*n.* 治療法

Question 46

什麼是風水？

What's Feng Shui?

Feng Shui is the Chinese system of geomancy.

It determines where to position graves, buildings and furniture.

Feng Shui can influence a person's fortune, health and relationships.

**

---

system ('sɪstəm) *n.* 體制；學說
geomancy ('dʒiə‚mænsɪ) *n.* 土占；地占
determine (dɪ'tɜmɪn) *v.* 決定
position (pə'zɪʃən) *v.* 把…置於（適當位置）
grave (grev) *n.* 墳墓   fortune ('fɔrtʃən) *n.* 運氣
relationship (rɪ'leʃən‚ʃɪp) *n.* 關係

【背景説明】

1. *What's Feng Shui?*

　　這句話的意思是「什麼是風水？」也可説成：
What does the term Feng Shui mean? (風水這
個名詞是什麼意思？)

2. *Feng Shui is the Chinese system of geomancy.*

geomancy (ˈdʒiəˌmænsɪ) *n.* 土占；地占

　　這句話的意思是「風水是中國的土占體系。」
也可説成：

Feng Shui is the Chinese art or practice of
positioning objects.
(風水是中國擺放物品的技巧或方法。)

Feng Shui is based on the flow of a force called
"chi." (風水是以一種稱爲『氣』的能量流動爲根據。)

Feng Shui 又稱爲 Chinese Geomancy。

flow (flo) *n.* 流動　　force (fors) *n.* 能量；力量
art (ɑrt) *n.* 方法；技巧　　practice (ˈpræktɪs) *n.* 做法

3. *It determines where to position graves, buildings and furniture.*

determine (dɪˈtɝmɪn) *v.* 決定
position (pəˈzɪʃən) *v.* 把…置於 (適當位置)
grave (grev) *n.* 墳墓

　　這句話的意思是「它決定墳墓、建築物和傢俱的擺
放位置。」也可説成：

Chinese position things like buildings
and furniture according to Feng Shui.

（中國人會根據風水放置物品，如建築物和傢俱。）

Feng Shui decides how and where to arrange
things.（風水決定安置物品的方式和位置。）

The laws of Feng Shui guide us on where to
position things.

（風水的原理指導我們擺放東西的位置。）

arrange〔ə'rendʒ〕v. 安排；佈置　　law〔lɔ〕n. 原理；定律
guide〔gaɪd〕v. 指引

4. ***Feng Shui can influence a person's fortune, health
and relationships.***
influence〔'ɪnfluəns〕v. 影響
fortune〔'fɔrtʃən〕n. 運氣
relationship〔rɪ'leʃən‚ʃɪp〕n. 關係

　　這句話的意思是「風水可能會影響一個人的運氣、
健康，以及與人的關係。」也可說成：

Feng Shui can be an influence in all areas
of a person's life.

（風水可能會對一個人生活的各方面產生影響。）

Feng Shui can really affect many aspects
of your life.

（風水可能真的會對你一生的許多方面產生影響。）

【area〔'ɛrɪə〕n. 方面　　aspect〔'æspɛkt〕n. 方面】

風水背後的理論是什麼？

What's the theory behind Feng Shui?

Its purpose is to create a harmonious relationship with the environment.

"Feng Shui" literally means "Wind and Water."

Wind and water are part of nature.

**────────────────

theory (ˈθiərɪ) *n.* 理論
behind (bɪˈhaɪnd) *prep.* 在…背後
create (krɪˈet) *v.* 創造
harmonious (harˈmonɪəs) *adj.* 和諧的
environment (ɪnˈvaɪrənmənt) *n.* 環境
literally (ˈlɪtərəlɪ) *adv.* 照字面義意地

【背景説明】

1. *What's the theory behind Feng Shui?*

   theory (ˈθiərɪ) *n.* 理論　behind (bɪˈhaɪnd) *prep.* 在…背後

   > 這句話的意思是「風水背後的理論是什麼？」也可説成：

   What's the underlying message of Feng Shui?
   （風水根本的含意是什麼？）

   Please tell me the main idea behind Feng Shui.
   （請告訴我風水背後的主要觀念。）

   underlying (ˈʌndəˌlaɪɪŋ) *adj.* 根本的；基本的
   message (ˈmɛsɪdʒ) *n.* 含意；主旨

   > behind 除了指人或物的位置「在…的後面」，亦
   > 可指隱藏在事物背後的涵義、原理等，如：There are
   > some allegories behind this story. (這故事背後隱藏
   > 了些寓意。)【allegory (ˈæləˌgorɪ) *n.* 寓言】

2. *Its purpose is to create a harmonious relationship
   with the environment.*

   purpose (ˈpɝpəs) *n.* 目的　create (krɪˈet) *v.* 創造
   harmonious (harˈmonɪəs) *adj.* 和諧的
   environment (ɪnˈvaɪrənmənt) *n.* 環境

   > 這句話的意思是「它的目的是創造與環境的和諧
   > 關係。」也可説成：

   The goal of Chinese Geomancy is to produce a
   harmonious environment.
   （風水的目的是製造一個和諧的環境。）

The idea behind Feng Shui is to establish
harmony in our everyday lives.

（風水背後的觀念是建立我們日常生活中的和諧。）

geomancy（ˈdʒiəˌmænsɪ）*n.* 土占；地占
establish（əˈstæblɪʃ）*v.* 建立

3. *"Feng Shui" literally means "Wind and Water."*

literally（ˈlɪtərəlɪ）*adv.* 照字面意義地

　　這句話的意思是「Feng Shui 的字面意義是『風和水』。」也可說成：

The literal meaning of Feng Shui is wind
and water.（Feng Shui 字面的意義是風和水。）

The exact meaning of Feng Shui is wind
and water.（Feng Shui 正確的意義是風和水。）

【literal（ˈlɪtərəl）*adj.* 照字面的　exact（ɪgˈzækt）*adj.* 正確的】

4. *Wind and water are part of nature.*

　　這句話的意思是「風和水是大自然的一部分。」
也可說成：

These two elements are essential parts of nature.

（這兩個元素是大自然不可或缺的一部分。）

Wind and water represent natural forces.

（風和水代表大自然的力量。）

element（ˈɛləmənt）*n.* 要素　essential（əˈsɛnʃəl）*adj.* 必要的
represent（ˌrɛprɪˈzɛnt）*v.* 代表

Question 48 為什麼太極拳這麼流行？

Why is Taijiquan so popular?

It's slow-motion shadowboxing.

It's a great way for anyone to keep in shape.

"Tai Chi" improves the lungs, digestion and muscle tone.

**

Taijiquan〔'taɪ'dʒi'kwɑn〕*n.* 太極拳
slow-motion〔'slo'moʃən〕*adj.* 慢動作的
shadowboxing〔'ʃædo͵bɑksɪŋ〕*n.*（與假想對手的）拳擊練習
keep in shape 保持健康　　improve〔ɪm'pruv〕*v.* 改善
lung〔lʌŋ〕*n.* 肺　　digestion〔də'dʒɛstʃən〕*n.* 消化
muscle〔'mʌsl̩〕*n.* 肌肉　　tone〔ton〕*n.* 健康的狀態

【背景説明】

1. ***Why is Taijiquan so popular?***

   Taijiquan (ˈtaɪˈdʒiˈkwɑn) *n.* 太極拳

   　　這句話的意思是「爲什麼太極拳這麼流行？」也可説成：

   Why do so many people practice Tai Chi Chuan?

   （爲什麼這麼多人打太極拳？）

   What are the benefits of tai chi?

   （太極拳的好處是什麼？）【benefit (ˈbɛnəfɪt) *n.* 好處】

   　　太極拳有很多種拼法：Taijiquan、Tai Chi Chuan、tai chi、tai chi quan…等，外國人大都知道有太極拳。

2. ***It's slow-motion shadowboxing.***

   slow-motion (ˈsloˈmoʃən) *adj.* 慢動作的

   shadowboxing (ˈʃædoˌbɑksɪŋ) *n.* (與假想對手的) 拳擊練習

   　　這句話的意思是「它是慢動作的拳擊練習。」也可説成：

   Tai Chi is a slow moving form of exercise.

   （太極拳是一種慢動作的運動形式。）

   It's designed especially for self defense and
   meditation. (它的目的特別是爲了自我防禦和冥想。)

   Tai Chi is a form of martial art.

   （太極拳是武術的一種。）

   martial (ˈmɑrʃəl) *adj.* 戰爭的；勇武的　***martial art*** 武術

   meditation (ˌmɛdəˈteʃən) *n.* 冥想

3. **It's a great way for anyone to keep in shape.**

    great〔gret〕*adj.* 很棒的   **keep in shape** 保持健康

    這句話的意思是「它對任何人而言，都是一種保持健康的好方法。」也可説成：

Practicing Tai Chi will keep you fit.
（打太極拳可以使你保持身體健康。）
Tai Chi strengthens your body and prevents
    disease.（太極拳可以強健你的身體，並預防疾病。）
【fit〔fɪt〕*adj.* 健康的   strengthen〔'stɛŋkθən〕*v.* 強化】

    in shape 是表示「健康狀況良好的」，keep in shape 和 keep fit 都是「保持健康」的口語用法。

4. **"Tai Chi" improves the lungs, digestion and muscle tone.**

    improve〔ɪm'pruv〕*v.* 改善   lung〔lʌŋ〕*n.* 肺
digestion〔də'dʒɛstʃən〕*n.* 消化
muscle〔'mʌsḷ〕*n.* 肌肉   tone〔ton〕*n.* 健康的狀態

    這句話的意思是「『太極拳』可以改善肺臟、消化，以及肌肉的狀態。」也可説成：

Tai qi quan strengthens muscles and your
    immune system.
（太極拳能強化肌肉和你的免疫系統。）
The exercises improves respiration, digestion
    and muscle tone.
（這種運動對呼吸、消化及肌肉的狀態都有幫助。）
immune〔ɪ'mjun〕*adj.* 免疫的
respiration〔ˌrɛspə'reʃən〕*n.* 呼吸

中國的生肖是關於些什麼？

What's the Chinese Zodiac all about?

The Chinese Zodiac is a twelve-year, twelve-animal cycle.

It's based on your birth year, not your birth month.

Many believe you have the animal characteristics of your birth year.

**

zodiac ('zodɪˌæk) *n.* (黃道) 十二宮
cycle ('saɪkḷ) *n.* 週期
be based on 以…爲基礎；根據　　birth (bɝθ) *n.* 出生
characteristic (ˌkærɪktə'rɪstɪk) *n.* 特性

【背景說明】

1. ***What's the Chinese Zodiac all about?***
zodiac（'zodɪ,æk) *n.* (黃道) 十二宮
Chinese Zodiac 中國的十二生肖

這句話的意思是「中國的生肖是關於些什麼？」
也可說成：Do you know anything about the Chinese
Zodiac?（你知道任何關於中國十二生肖的事嗎？）

黃道帶是指日、月及主要行星運行的地帶，分爲
十二宮（sign）。在西方，每一宮代表一個星座，以
出生月來決定你所屬的星座；在中國，每一宮代表一
種動物，以出生年來決定你所屬的生肖動物。

2. ***The Chinese Zodiac is a twelve-year, twelve-animal cycle.***
cycle（'saɪkḷ) *n.* 週期

這句話的意思是「中國的十二生肖是一個十二年、
十二種動物的循環週期。」也可說成：

Ancient Chinese astrologers divided the
years into a twelve-animal cycle.
（中國古代的占星專家將十二年分成十二種動物的
循環週期。）

Each year, for twelve years, a different
animal represents the year.
（十二年中的每一年，都有不同的動物作代表。）

ancient（'enʃənt) *adj.* 古代的
astrologer (ə'strɑlədʒɚ) *n.* 占星家　　divide (də'vaɪd) *v.* 劃分

3. ***It's based on your birth year, not your birth month.***
   be based on 根據；以～為基礎　　birth〔bɝθ〕*n.* 出生

   　　這句話的意思是「它是根據你的出生年，而非出生的月份。」也可以說：

   Unlike that of the west, the Chinese Zodiac is
   based on years not months.
   （不同於西方國家，中國的十二生肖是根據年，而非月。）

   Your fortune depends on the year you were
   born, not the month.
   （你的命運是取決於你的出生年，而非出生月。）

   fortune（'fɔrtʃən）*n.* 運氣；命運
   depend on 視～而定；取決於

4. ***Many believe you have the animal characteristics
   of your birth year.***
   characteristic〔ˌkærɪktə'rɪstɪk〕*n.* 特性

   　　這句話的意思是「許多人相信，你擁有你出生年動物的特性。」也可說成：

   It is commonly believed that you inherit the
   traits of the animal year you were born in.
   （人們普遍相信，你繼承了你出生年動物的特性。）

   Taiwanese think that you acquire the qualities
   of the animal.（台灣人認為你會得到該動物的特性。）

   inherit〔ɪn'hɛrɪt〕*v.* 繼承　　trait〔tret〕*n.* 特性
   acquire〔ə'kwaɪr〕*v.* 獲得　　quality（'kwɑlətɪ）*n.* 特性

50

麻將怎麼打？

How do you play mah-jong?

It's like playing bridge but with
    dominoes instead of cards.

Playing mah-jong requires a square
    table and four people.

To win you must get 17 tiles and
    arrange them in order.

**

mah-jong (maˊdʒɔŋ) *n.* 麻將
bridge (brɪdʒ) *n.* 橋牌　domino (ˊdɑməˏno) *n.* 骨牌
instead of 而不是　require (rɪˊkwaɪr) *v.* 需要
square (skwɛr) *adj.* 正方形的　tile (taɪl) *n.* (麻將的) 牌
arrange (əˊrendʒ) *v.* 排列　***in order*** 按照順序

【背景説明】

1. *How do you play mah-jong?*
   mah-jong〔maˈdʒɔŋ〕*n.* 麻將

> 這句話的意思是「麻將怎麼打？」也可説成：

Can you tell me the rules for playing mah-jong?
（你可以告訴我打麻將的規則嗎？）

Could you fill me in on how to play mah-jong?
（你可以詳細告訴我怎麼打麻將嗎？）

【*fill sb. in on* sth. 詳細告訴某人某事】

2. *It's like playing bridge but with dominoes instead of cards.*
   bridge〔brɪdʒ〕*n.* 橋牌　　domino〔ˈdamə͵no〕*n.* 骨牌
   instead of 而不是　　card〔kard〕*n.* 紙牌

> 這句話的意思是「它很像打橋牌，但是用骨牌代替紙牌。」也可説成：

It's similar to card games like bridge or rummy.
（它類似紙牌遊戲，像是橋牌或拉米牌戲。）

In mah-jong solid pieces or tiles are used,
　not cards.
（麻將使用的是實心的棋子或牌，而不是紙牌。）

solid〔ˈsalɪd〕*adj.* 實心的　　piece〔pis〕*n.* 一塊；棋子
tile〔taɪl〕*n.* (麻將的) 牌　　rummy〔ˈrʌmɪ〕*n.* 拉米牌戲

3. ***Playing mah-jong requires a square table and four people.***

require (rɪˋkwaɪr) v. 需要

square (skwɛr) *adj.* 正方形的

這句話的意思是「打麻將需要一張正方形的桌子和四個人。」也可說成：

A square table is needed and four participants, too.

（一張正方形的桌子是必需的，四個參與者也是必要的。）

You can't play mah-jong unless you have four people and a four side table.

（除非有四個人和一張四邊桌，否則你沒辦法打麻將。）

【participant (pɚˋtɪsəpənt) *n.* 參與者】

4. ***To win you must get 17 tiles and arrange them in order.***

tile (taɪl) *n.* (麻將的) 牌　　arrange (əˋrendʒ) *v.* 排列

in order 按照順序

這句話的意思是「要贏你必須要拿到十七張牌，並且依順序排列。」也可說成：

Get 17 pieces, organize them in succession of threes and a two and you win!

（拿到十七張牌，組織它們成連續三張和連續二張，然後你就贏了！）

【organize (ˋɔrgənˏaɪz) *v.* 組織；使有條理】

Question 51　什麼時候慶祝中國新年？

When is Chinese New Year celebrated?

Most holidays in Taiwan are celebrated according to the lunar calendar.

This traditional calendar changes from year to year.

New Year's could be any date between mid-January and late February.

**

celebrate (ˈsɛləˌbret) v. 慶祝　***according to*** 根據
lunar (ˈlunɚ) *adj.* 月亮的　　calendar (ˈkæləndɚ) *n.* 日曆
lunar calendar 陰曆；農曆
traditional (trəˈdɪʃənḷ) *adj.* 傳統的
mid- (mɪd) 表「…的中間」　late (let) *adj.* 末期的
New Year's 新年；初一 (= *New Year's Day*)

【背景說明】

1. ***When is Chinese New Year celebrated?***

   celebrate〔ˈsɛləˌbret〕*v.* 慶祝

   　　這句話的意思是「什麼時候慶祝中國新年？」也
   可説成：What date does the traditional Chinese
   New Year fall on?（中國傳統新年是在什麼日期？）

   　　【fall〔fɔl〕*v.*（節日、季節）適逢】

2. ***Most holidays in Taiwan are celebrated according to the***
   lunar calendar.

   according to 根據　　lunar〔ˈlunɚ〕*adj.* 月亮的
   calendar〔ˈkæləndɚ〕*n.* 日曆　　***lunar calendar*** 陰曆；農曆

   　　這句話的意思是「大部分台灣節日的慶祝是根據陰曆。」
   也可説成：

   Many traditional holidays in Taiwan are
   celebrated on lunar calendar dates.
   （許多傳統的台灣節日通常都在陰曆的日期慶祝。）
   Holidays in Taiwan are usually determined by the
   lunar calendar.（台灣的節日通常以陰曆決定。）

   　　【determine〔dɪˈtɝmɪn〕*v.* 決定】

3. *This traditional calendar changes from year to year.*

　　這句話的意思是「這個傳統的日曆年年改變。」也可說成：

The lunar calendar changes every year, in
　　contrast to the solar calendar.

（相對於陽曆，陰曆每年都會改變。）

A lunar month is slightly shorter than a solar
　　calendar month.

（陰曆一個月比陽曆一個月稍微短一些。）

solar（'solæ）*adj.* 太陽的　　*solar calendar* 陽曆
contrast（'kɑntræst）*n.* 對照　　slightly（'slaɪtlɪ）*adv.* 稍微地

4. *New Year's could be any date between mid-January
and late February.*

date（det）*n.* 日期　　mid-（mɪd）…的中間

　　這句話的意思是「新年可能是一月中到二月底間的任何一天。」也可說成：

Chinese New Year is in either January or
　　February.（中國新年不是在一月就是在二月。）

The Taiwanese celebrate New Year in January
　　or February.

（台灣人在一月或二月慶祝新年。）

　　New Year's 是 New Year's Day 的簡寫，指的是新年的第一天（初一）而非整個新年假期。月初、月中及月底的表現方式分別為：early～、mid-～、late～。

52 台灣人如何慶祝農曆新年？

How do Taiwanese celebrate the Lunar New Year?

Families have dinner together on New Year's Eve.

Adults give "hung-bao" to parents and children.

We wear new clothes, renew red-paper couplets and set off firecrackers.

** ─────────────────────

celebrate〔'sɛlə͵bret〕*v.* 慶祝
Lunar New Year 農曆新年　　eve〔iv〕*n.* 前夕
adult〔ə'dʌlt〕*n.* 成人　　renew〔rɪ'nju〕*v.* 更新
couplet〔'kʌplɪt〕*n.*（詩）對句　***red-paper couplet*** 春聯
set off 燃放　　firecracker〔'faɪr͵krækə〕*n.* 鞭炮

【背景說明】

1. ***How do Taiwanese celebrate the Lunar New Year?***

   celebrate (ˈsɛlə،bret) *v.* 慶祝

   lunar (ˈlunɚ) *adj.* 月亮的

   Lunar New Year 農曆新年 (= *Chinese New Year*)

   這句話的意思是「台灣人如何慶祝農曆新年？」也
   可說成：

   How is the Chinese New Year celebrated in
   Taiwan? (在台灣如何慶祝農曆新年？)

   What do the Taiwanese do to enjoy the New
   Year holiday?

   (台灣人會做什麼來享受新年假期？)

2. ***Families have dinner together on New Year's Eve.***

   eve (iv) *n.* 前夕　***New Year's Eve*** 除夕

   這句話的意思是「家人會在除夕一起吃晚餐。」
   也可說成：

   One major custom is to eat a big feast with
   family on New Year's Eve.

   (有個主要的風俗是，在除夕和家人一起吃大餐。)

   All family members must return home to
   feast together.

   (所有的家庭成員必須回家一起吃大餐。)

   major (ˈmedʒɚ) *adj.* 主要的

   feast (fist) *n.* 盛宴　*v.* 飽餐；大吃

3. ***Adults give "hung-bao" to parents and children.***
adult〔ə'dʌlt〕*n.* 成人

這句話的意思是「成年人給父母和小孩紅包。」

也可說成：Red envelopes with money inside are given
to children and parents by all adults. (裡面有裝錢的紅
包是由成年人給小孩和父母。)【envelope〔'ɛnvə,lop〕*n.* 信封】

4. ***We wear new clothes, renew red-paper couplets***
and set off firecrackers.
renew〔rɪ'nju〕*v.* 更新　　couplet〔'kʌplɪt〕*n.* (詩) 對句
set off 燃放　　firecracker〔'faɪr,krækɚ〕*n.* 鞭炮

這句話的意思是「我們穿新衣、換新春聯，並且
放鞭炮。」也可說成：

People celebrate by wearing new outfits.
(人們藉由穿整套的新衣來慶祝。)

Everyone also likes to stick up red couplets
on their front doors.
(大家也喜歡在門口貼上紅色的對聯。)

Firecrackers are set off to scare away a
traditional legendary monster named Nian.
(放鞭炮是為了嚇跑古老傳說中名叫「年」的怪獸。)

firecracker 也可以用 cracker 取代，都是指「爆
竹」；而 firework 是「煙火」。

outfit〔'aʊt,fɪt〕*n.* 整套服裝　　scare〔skɛr〕*v.* 驚嚇
legendary〔'lɛdʒənd,ɛrɪ〕*adj.* 傳說的

什麼是「紅包」？

What is a "hung-bao"?

It's a red envelope with money inside.

In Chinese culture, red is a lucky color.

Red envelopes will bring luck to the giver and the receiver.

**

envelope ('εnvə,lop) *n.* 信封
culture ('kʌltʃə) *v.* 文化
lucky ('lʌkɪ) *adj.* 幸運的　luck (lʌk) *n.* 幸運；運氣
giver ('gɪvə) *n.* 給予者
receiver (rɪ'sivə) *n.* 接受者

【背景説明】

1. ***What is a "hung-bao"?***

這句話的意思是「什麼是『紅包』？」也可説成：

Can you please explain what a "hung-bao" is?

（可以請你說明什麼是紅包嗎？）

【explain〔ɪkˈsplen〕v. 說明】

2. ***It's a red envelope with money inside.***

envelope〔ˈɛnvəˌlop〕n. 信封

這句話的意思是「它是一個裡面有錢的紅色信封。」
也可説成：

A hung-bao is a red, cash-filled envelope.

（紅包是裝了現金的紅色信封。）

The most popular and welcome gift for
　　Chinese is the red envelope filled with
　　money, called a "hung-bao."

（對中國人來說，最普遍且最受歡迎的禮
　物，就是裝了錢的紅色信封，稱為紅包。）

welcome〔ˈwɛlkəm〕adj. 受歡迎的　　fill〔fɪl〕v. 裝
gift〔gɪft〕n. 禮物

3. *In Chinese culture, red is a lucky color.*

culture (ˈkʌltʃɚ) *v.* 文化　　lucky (ˈlʌkɪ) *adj.* 幸運的

這句話的意思是「在中國文化中，紅色是幸運的顏色。」也可說成：Red is considered an auspicious color by Chinese. (中國人視紅色爲吉利的顏色。)

【auspicious (ɔˈspɪʃəs) *adj.* 吉利的 】

4. *Red envelopes will bring luck to the giver and the receiver.*

luck (lʌk) *n.* 幸運；運氣　　giver (ˈgɪvɚ) *n.* 給予者
receiver (rɪˈsivɚ) *n.* 接受者

這句話的意思是「紅包會爲給予者及接受者帶來幸運。」也可說成：

Both the giver and receiver of the "hung-bao" will have good luck.
(紅包的給予者和接受者都會有好運氣。)

It's believed that both the giver and the receiver will enjoy good luck.
(人們相信給予者和接受者都會得到好運。)

Red envelopes bring luck and fortune to those that give and receive them.
(紅包帶給給予及收受它們的人幸運及財富。)

enjoy (ɪnˈdʒɔɪ) *v.* 享有　　fortune (ˈfɔrtʃən) *n.* 財富
receive (rɪˈsiv) *v.* 領受

什麼是端午節？

What is the Dragon Boat Festival?

It's a holiday on the fifth day of the fifth lunar month.

It's in memory of Chu Yuan, and we also call it Poet's Day.

We have dragon boat races and eat Chung-tze on this day.

**

dragon (ˈdrægən) *n.* 龍　　*dragon boat* 龍舟
festival (ˈfɛstəvl̩) *n.* 節日；節慶
Dragon Boat Festival 端午節　　*in memory of* 紀念
Chu Yuan 屈原　　poet (ˈpoɪt) *n.* 詩人
race (res) *n.* 競賽　　*Chung-tze* 粽子

【背景説明】

1. ***What is the Dragon Boat Festival?***
   dragon (ˈdrægən) *n.* 龍　***dragon boat*** 龍舟
   festival (ˈfɛstəvl̩) *n.* 節日；節慶
   Dragon Boat Festival 端午節

   這句話的意思是「什麼是端午節？」也可説成：
   How do Taiwanese celebrate the Dragon Boat
   Festival? (台灣人怎麼慶祝端午節？)

2. ***It's a holiday on the fifth day of the fifth lunar month.***

   這句話的意思是「它是在農曆五月五日的一個節
   日。」也可説成：

   This traditional holiday falls on May 5th
   of the lunar calendar.
   （這個傳統的假日是在農曆五月五日。）

   The popular holiday occurs in the fifth
   month of the lunar year.
   （這個受歡迎的假日是在農曆五月。）

   【*fall on* 適逢】

3. *It's in memory of Chu Yuan, and we also call it*
   Poet's Day.
   in memory of 紀念　poet〔'poɪt〕*n.* 詩人

   這句話的意思是「它是爲了紀念屈原，我們又稱
   它爲詩人節。」也可説成：On the Dragon Boat
   Festival we commemorate the poet Chu Yuan.
   （在端午節我們紀念詩人屈原。）
   【commemorate〔kə'mɛmə,ret〕*v.* 紀念】

4. *We have dragon boat races and eat Chung-tze on this day*.
   dragon boat race 龍舟競賽
   race〔res〕*n.* 競賽　*Chung-tze* 粽子

   這句話的意思是「在這天我們舉行龍舟競賽並吃粽
   子。」也可説成：

   Two popular customs on this day are dragon
   boat racing and eating rice dumplings.
   （在這天有兩個受歡迎的風俗，那就是龍舟賽和吃粽子。）
   dumpling〔'dʌmplɪŋ〕*n.* 呈塊狀或糰狀的食物
   rice dumpling 粽子

   dumpling 是指呈塊狀或糰狀的食物，所以如餃子
   （Chinese dumplings）、湯圓（rice-flour dumplings）、
   肉圓（round dumpling with meat）等，都用 dumpling
   這個字。很多食物都叫 rice dumpling，若想清楚表達粽子，
   可以在前面加上 glutinous（glutinous rice 糯米）。
   【glutinous〔'glutɪnəs〕*adj.* 黏的】

55　什麼是中秋節？

What's the Mid-Autumn Festival?

It's a traditional family "reunion" holiday.

It's a celebration of the moon at its fullest and brightest.

The full moon is a great time for reflection and romance.

** ─────────────────

Mid-Autumn Festival 中秋節
traditional (trə'dɪʃənl̩) *adj.* 傳統的
reunion (ri'junjən) *n.* 團圓
celebration (ˌsɛlə'breʃən) *n.* 慶祝會
full moon 滿月　　reflection (rɪ'flɛkʃən) *n.* 深思；內省
romance (ro'mæns) *n.* 浪漫氣氛

【背景説明】

1. ***What's the Mid-Autumn Festival?***

    這句話的意思是「什麼是中秋節？」也可説成：

    Why do Taiwanese celebrate the "Moon Festival?" (爲什麼台灣人要慶祝中秋節？)

    What customs are practiced during the Mid-Autumn Festival? (在中秋節有什麼風俗？)

    What do people do on the Moon Festival?

    (人們在中秋節都做些什麼事？)

2. ***It's a traditional family "reunion" holiday.***
    traditional〔 trə'dɪʃənḷ〕*adj.* 傳統的
    reunion〔 ri'junjən〕*n.* 團圓

    這句話的意思是「它是一個傳統的家庭團圓節日。」
    也可以説：

    The Moon Festival is a great time for families to get together. (中秋節是一個家人團聚的重要時刻。)

    Everybody enjoys eating delicious moon cakes.
    (每個人都享用美味的月餅。)

    Many families today like to barbeque outside or have a big feast.

    (現在許多家庭都喜歡在外面烤肉或吃一頓大餐。)

    moon cake 月餅　barbeque〔'barbɪ͵kju〕*v.* 烤肉
    feast〔 fist〕*n.* 盛宴

3. *It's a celebration of the moon at it's fullest and brightest.*
   celebration (,sɛlə'breʃən) *n.* 慶祝會
   full (fʊl) *adj.* 滿的　　bright (braɪt) *adj.* 明亮的

   這句話的意思是「它是一個在月亮最圓最亮時的慶
   祝活動。」也可說成：

   The moon has great significance and deep
   meaning for Chinese.
   （月亮對中國人而言意義重大，而且意涵深遠。）

   The Chinese culture has celebrated the moon
   for thousands of years.
   （中國文化對月亮的歌頌已經數千年了。）

   【significance (sɪg'nɪfəkəns) *n.* 意義重大；重要性】

4. *The full moon is a great time for reflection and romance.*
   full moon 滿月　　reflection (rɪ'flɛkʃən) *n.* 深思；內省
   romance (ro'mæns) *n.* 浪漫氣氛

   這句話的意思是「滿月是一個深思默想及充滿浪漫
   情調的重要時刻。」也可說成：

   Staring at the full moon is romantic and relaxing.
   （凝視滿月是浪漫而輕鬆的。）

   Many legends like the Chang O story inspire
   people to think about love.
   （許多傳說，例如嫦娥的故事，會激發人們思考關於愛的事。）

   stare (stɛr) *v.* 凝視　　relax (rɪ'læks) *v.* 放鬆
   legend ('lɛdʒənd) *n.* 傳說　　inspire (ɪn'spaɪr) *v.* 激發

Question 56 你們有像萬聖節前夕的節日嗎？

Do you have any holidays like Halloween?

The seventh lunar month is called "ghost month."

The gates of hell open up and ghosts roam the earth.

People hold "Pudu" rites to appease the ghosts.

**

Halloween〔ˌhæloˈin〕*n.* 萬聖節前夕　　ghost〔gost〕*n.* 鬼

gate〔get〕*n.* 大門　　hell〔hɛl〕*n.* 地獄

roam〔rom〕*v.* 在～遊蕩　　hold〔hold〕*v.* 舉行

rite〔raɪt〕*n.* 儀式　　appease〔əˈpiz〕*v.* 撫慰

【背景説明】

1. *Do you have any holidays like Halloween?*
   Halloween〔͵hælo'in〕*n.* 萬聖節前夕

   　　這句話的意思是「你們有像萬聖節前夕的節日嗎？」
   也可説成：Is there any holiday or festival in Taiwan
   concerning ghosts?（台灣有任何假日或節日是和鬼有關
   的嗎？）

   　　11 月 1 日萬聖節（All Saints' Day）是西方的鬼
   節，小朋友會在 10 月 31 日萬聖節前夕（Halloween）
   扮鬼，挨家挨戶要糖吃，他們會説：Trick or treat!
   （不給糖，就搗蛋！）

   concerning〔kən'sɜnɪŋ〕*prep.* 關於　　saint〔sent〕*n.* 聖徒
   trick〔trɪk〕*n.* 惡作劇　　treat〔trit〕*n.* 請客

2. *The seventh lunar month is called "ghost month."*
   the seventh lunar month 農曆七月　　ghost〔gost〕*n.* 鬼

   　　這句話的意思是「農曆七月被稱爲『鬼月』。」也
   可説成：

   Taiwan has a "ghost month" during the seventh
   　　lunar month.（台灣的農曆七月是『鬼月』。）
   Ghost month has several important rules, like
   　　no moving, no traveling and no marriage,
   　　that you must follow.
   　　（鬼月有幾個重要的慣例你必須要遵守，像是不搬家、
   　　　不旅行，和不結婚。）
   【moving〔'muvɪŋ〕*n.* 搬家　　follow〔'falo〕*v.* 遵守】

3. *The gates of hell open up and ghosts roam the earth*.

gate〔get〕*n.* 大門　　hell〔hɛl〕*n.* 地獄
roam〔rom〕*v.* 在～遊蕩

這句話的意思是「地獄的門打開，讓鬼在人間遊蕩。」還可說這句話來補充說明：

We call these wandering souls "good brothers."
（我們稱這些遊蕩的鬼魂『好兄弟』。）
【wander〔'wɑndɚ〕*v.* 遊蕩　　soul〔sol〕*n.* 靈魂】

4. *People hold "Pudu" rites to appease the ghosts*.

rite〔raɪt〕*n.* 儀式　　appease〔ə'piz〕*v.* 撫慰

這句話的意思是「人們舉行『普渡』儀式來撫慰這些鬼魂。」也可說成：

This ceremony entails rich offerings for
ghosts and much burning of paper money.
（這儀式會有豐盛的祭品給鬼魂享用，並焚燒很多
的紙錢。）

A "Pudu" rite is offering rich sacrifices
and burning a lot of paper money for ghosts.
（『普渡』儀式是供奉豐盛的祭品和燒很多紙錢給
鬼魂。）

ceremony〔'sɛrə,monɪ〕*n.* 儀式
entail〔ɪn'tel〕*v.* 必然伴有… 　　offering〔'ɔfərɪŋ〕*n.* 祭品
sacrifice〔'sækrə,faɪs〕*n.* 祭品

台灣人如何祭拜祖先？

How do Taiwanese worship
their ancestors?

We go to their tombs on Tomb
Sweeping Day, April 5th.

We repair and clean the tomb and set
out a feast for our ancestors.

It's an expression of filial respect for
our forebears.

＊＊

worship（ˋwɝʃəp）v. 祭拜　　ancestor（ˋænsɛstɚ）n. 祖先
tomb（tum）n. 墳墓　***Tomb Sweeping Day*** 掃墓節（清明節）
feast（fist）n. 筵席　　expression（ɪkˋsprɛʃən）n. 表現
filial（ˋfɪlɪəl）*adj.* 子女的　　forebear（ˋforˌbɛr）n. 祖先

【背景說明】

1. *How do Taiwanese worship their ancestors?*

worship〔ˈwɝʃəp〕v. 祭拜　ancestor〔ˈænsɛstɚ〕n. 祖先

這句話的意思是「台灣人如何祭拜祖先？」也可說成：

In what ways do Taiwanese worship their
ancestors?（台灣人用什麼方式祭拜他們的祖先？）

How do Taiwanese commemorate their dead
ancestors?（台灣人如何紀念他們死去的祖先？）

【commemorate〔kəˈmɛməˌret〕v. 紀念】

2. *We go to their tombs on Tomb Sweeping Day, April 5ᵗʰ.*

tomb〔tum〕n. 墳墓　*Tomb Sweeping Day* 掃墓節（清明節）

這句話的意思是「我們在四月五日清明節前往他們
的墳墓。」也可說成：

Every April 5ᵗʰ, Taiwanese visit their family
tombs to pray for loved ones.
（每年的四月五日，台灣人會前去探望他們家人的墓，
並為親人祈禱。）

The Chinese are very respectful of their ancestors,
so this holiday is set according to the solar calendar.
（中國人很尊敬祖先，所以根據陽曆訂定了這個節日。）

pray〔pre〕v. 祈禱　*loved ones* 親人
solar〔ˈsolɚ〕adj. 太陽的

3. *We repair and clean the tomb and set out a feast for our ancestors.*

repair〔rɪ'pɛr〕*v.* 修理　　*set out* 擺出（食物）

feast〔fist〕*n.* 盛宴

　　　這句話的意思是「我們整修清理墳墓，並爲我們的祖先擺出豐盛的食物。」也可說成：

Tomb Sweeping Day is a grave cleaning day.

（清明節是一個清理墳墓的日子。）

Taiwanese cut grass, burn grass and pull
　　weeds on family graves.

（台灣人爲親人的墓割草、燒草，以及拔雜草。）

grave〔grev〕*n.* 墳墓　　grass〔græs〕*n.* 草

pull〔pʊl〕*v.* 拔　　weed〔wid〕*n.* 雜草

4. *It's an expression of filial respect for our forebears.*

expression〔ɪk'sprɛʃən〕*n.* 表現

filial〔'fɪlɪəl〕*adj.* 子女的　　forebear〔'for,bɛr〕*n.* 祖先

　　　這句話的意思是「它是子女對祖先尊敬的表現。」
也可說成：

Visiting family graves on Tomb Sweeping
　　Day is a traditional sign of respect.

（在清明節探望親人的墳墓，是一種傳統的尊敬
　　的表現。）

【sign〔saɪn〕*n.* 表示】

58 夜市有什麼特別的地方？

What's special about the night market?

The night market is one of the most exciting spots in Taiwan.

There are games to play, foods to eat and things to buy.

It represents the spirit of Taiwanese and their way of life.

**

exciting (ɪk'saɪtɪŋ) *adj.* 令人興奮的；刺激的；好玩的
spot (spɑt) *n.* 地方
represent (,rɛprɪ'zɛnt) *v.* 代表
spirit ('spɪrɪt) *n.* 精神

【背景説明】

1. ***What's so special about the night market?***
   night market 夜市

   　　　　這句話的意思是「夜市有什麼特別的地方？」也可
   說成：

   　　　　Why are the night markets so popular?
   　　　　（爲什麼夜市這麼受歡迎？）

   　　　　What is it about the night markets that
   　　　　　　make them so special?
   　　　　（夜市有些什麼特點使它們如此特別？）

2. ***The night market is one of the most exciting***
   spots in Taiwan.
   exciting〔ɪk'saɪtɪŋ〕*adj.* 令人興奮的；刺激的；好玩的
   spot〔spɑt〕*n.* 地方

   　　　　這句話的意思是「夜市是台灣最好玩的地方
   之一。」也可說成：

   　　　　The night markets are bustling with
   　　　　　　buyers and sellers.
   　　　　（夜市擠滿了購買者和銷售者。）

   　　　　The night market atmosphere is like a
   　　　　　　carnival.（夜市的氣氛就像是嘉年華會。）

   bustle〔'bʌsḷ〕*v.* 充滿　　atmosphere〔'ætməs,fɪr〕*n.* 氣氛
   carnival〔'kɑrnəvḷ〕*n.* 嘉年華會

3. ***There are games to play, foods to eat and things to buy.***

這句話的意思是「可以玩遊戲、吃東西,和買東西。」也可說成:

There are many things to do including eating, shopping and playing games.
(有很多事情可做,包括吃東西、買東西,和玩遊戲。)

There is something for everyone at a Taiwanese night market.
(台灣夜市能滿足每個人的需求。)

4. ***They represent the spirit of Taiwanese and their way of life.***

represent (͵rɛprɪˊzɛnt) v. 代表　　spirit (ˊspɪrɪt) n. 精神

這句話的意思是「它們代表了台灣人的精神和生活方式。」也可說成:

Night markets reflect the spirit of the Taiwanese people. (夜市反映了台灣人民的精神。)

The night markets are full of energetic people trying to make money and others looking for good bargains.
(夜市充滿了精力充沛、想賺錢的人,以及一些在尋找便宜貨的人。)

reflect (rɪˊflɛkt) v. 反映
energetic (͵ɛnɚˊdʒɛtɪk) adj. 充滿活力的
bargain (ˊbɑrgɪn) n. 廉價的交易;便宜貨

Question 59 哪裡是台灣最適合遊覽的地方？

What's the best place to visit in Taiwan?

Kenting National Park is a paradise for a vacation.

Kenting has many diverse ecosystems all in one place.

Kenting has Taiwan's largest collection of wildlife, marine life and plant life.

** ──────────────

paradise (ˈpærəˌdaɪs) *n.* 天堂
diverse (dəˈvɝs , daɪ-) *adj.* 各種的
ecosystem (ˈikoˌsɪstəm) *n.* 生態系統
collection (kəˈlɛkʃən) *n.* 收藏
marine (məˈrin) *adj.* 海洋的   life (laɪf) *n.* 生物

【背景説明】

1. ***What's the best place to visit in Taiwan?***

　　　　這句話的意思是「哪裡是台灣最適合遊覽的地方？」
也可說成：

Where is Taiwan's number one tourist spot?
（哪裡是台灣最棒的觀光勝地？）

Can you tell me a great place to visit in Taiwan?
（你可以告訴我一個台灣很值得遊覽的地方嗎？）

Which tourist spot in Taiwan is a "must see"?
（台灣哪一個觀光勝地是一定要去的？）

tourist (ˈturɪst) *adj.* 觀光的　　spot (spɑt) *n.* 地點
must see (ˈmʌstˌsi) *n.* 非看不可的地方

2. ***Kenting National Park is a paradise for a vacation.***
paradise (ˈpærəˌdaɪs) *n.* 天堂
vacation (veˈkeʃən) *n.* 假期

　　　　這句話的意思是「墾丁國家公園是一個度假天堂。」
也可說成：

Kenting National Park is the perfect place to
visit. (墾丁國家公園是一個完美的觀光地。)

Most visitors to Taiwan rate Kenting National
Park number one!
（大部分來台灣的觀光客認為墾丁國家公園是最好的！）

【perfect (ˈpɝfɪkt) *adj.* 完美的　　rate (ret) *v.* 評價；認為】

3. ***Kenting has many diverse ecosystems all in one place.***
diverse〔dəˈvɝs , daɪˈ-〕*adj.* 各種的
ecosystem〔ˈiko͵sɪstəm〕*n.* 生態系統

　　這句話的意思是「墾丁這個地方有許多各種的生態系統。」也可説成：

Kenting has forests, beaches, coral reefs
and grasslands all in one place.
（墾丁這個地方有森林、海灘、珊瑚礁和草原。）

The scenery around Kenting is diverse
and magnificent.
（墾丁周圍的風景是多樣而且壯麗的。）

coral〔ˈkɑrəl〕*adj.* 珊瑚的　　reef〔rif〕*n.* 礁
grassland〔ˈgræs͵lænd〕*n.* 草原　　scenery〔ˈsinərɪ〕*n.* 風景
magnificent〔mægˈnɪfəsn̩t〕*adj.* 壯麗的

4. ***Kenting has Taiwan's largest collection of wildlife,***
marine life and plant life.
collection〔kəˈlɛkʃən〕*n.* 收藏
wildlife〔ˈwaɪld͵laɪf〕*n.* 野生動物
marine〔məˈrin〕*adj.* 海洋的　　life〔laɪf〕*n.* 生物

　　這句話的意思是「墾丁有台灣最多的野生動物、海洋生物，以及植物。」也可説成：Kenting has a wide
variety of plant, animal and marine life.（墾丁有很多各種各樣的植物、動物，及海洋生物。）

　　【*a variety of* 各種的】

Question 60 哪裡是北台灣最棒的觀光景點？

What is the best sightseeing spot in northern Taiwan?

Yangmingshan National Park is the best choice.

It's famous for its hot springs and forest trails.

The best time to visit is the springtime, when everything is in bloom.

** ─────────────

sightseeing ('saɪt,siɪŋ) *adj.* 觀光的
northern ('nɔrðən) *adj.* 北部的　　***hot spring*** 溫泉
trail (trel) *n.* 小徑　　springtime ('sprɪŋ,taɪm) *n.* 春季
bloom (blum) *n.* 開花（期）

【背景説明】

1. ***What is the best sightseeing spot in northern Taiwan?***

   sightseeing (ˈsaɪtˌsiɪŋ) *adj.* 觀光的

   northern (ˈnɔrðən) *adj.* 北部的

   　　這句話的意思是「哪裡是北台灣最棒的觀光景點？」
   也可説成：What tourist spot in northern Taiwan
   do you recommend the most? (你最推薦北台灣什麼
   觀光景點？)【recommend (ˌrɛkəˈmɛnd) *v.* 推薦】

2. ***Yangmingshan National Park is the best choice.***

   　　這句話的意思是「陽明山國家公園是最好的選擇。」
   也可説成：

   Yangmingshan is the most popular spot.

   (陽明山是最受歡迎的景點。)

   Most people agree that "Yangming Mountain"
   is northern Taiwan's best spot.

   (大部分的人都同意『陽明山』是北台灣最好的景點。)

3. ***It's famous for its hot springs and forest trails.***

   famous (ˈfeməs) *adj.* 有名的

   spring (sprɪŋ) *n.* 泉水　　***hot spring*** 溫泉

   forest (ˈfɔrɪst) *n.* 森林　　trail (trel) *n.* 小徑

   　　這句話的意思是「它以溫泉及森林小徑聞名。」也
   可説成：

There are excellent hot springs and hiking
trails on Yangming Mountain.
（陽明山有很棒的溫泉和健行步道。）

excellent (ˈɛkslənt) *adj.* 極佳的
hiking (ˈhaɪkɪŋ) *n.* 健行；徒步旅行

4. ***The best time to visit is the springtime, when
everything is in bloom.***
springtime (ˈsprɪŋˌtaɪm) *n.* 春季
bloom (blum) *n.* 開花（期）

這句話的意思是「最好的觀光時機是春季，那時
所有的花都開了。」也可以說：

When its cherry trees and azalea blossom in
the spring, the park is full of visitors.
（當它的櫻花樹和杜鵑花在春天盛開時，這座公園
擠滿了觀光客。）

The spring flower blooming season is the
high season.
（春花盛開的季節是旺季。）

azalea (əˈzeljə) *n.* 杜鵑花　blossom (ˈblɑsəm) *v.* 開花
be full of 充滿了…　blooming (ˈblumɪŋ) *adj.* 開花的
high season 旺季（↔ *low season* 淡季）

哪裡是東台灣最棒的觀光景點？

What is the best sightseeing spot in eastern Taiwan?

Taroko Gorge is the most famous spot.

It is a gorge of marble cliffs forming a long valley.

The Central Cross Island Highway can lead you to its wonders.

**

eastern (ˈistən) *adj.* 東方的　　gorge (gɔrdʒ) *n.* 峽谷
marble (ˈmɑrbḷ) *adj.* 大理石的　　cliff (klɪf) *n.* 懸崖；峭壁
form (fɔrm) *v.* 形成　　valley (ˈvælɪ) *n.* 山谷
the Central Cross Island Highway 中部橫貫公路
lead (lid) *v.* (路) 帶引 (至…)
wonder (ˈwʌndə) *n.* 奇觀

【背景説明】

1. ***What is the best sightseeing spot in eastern Taiwan?***
eastern ('istən) *adj.* 東方的

　　這句話的意思是「哪裡是東台灣最棒的觀光景點？」
也可説成：Which tourist area in eastern Taiwan
should I visit?（我應該去東台灣的哪個觀光地區？）

2. ***Taroko Gorge is the most famous spot.***
gorge (gɔrdʒ) *n.* 峽谷

　　這句話的意思是「太魯閣峽谷是最有名的景點。」
也可説成：The jewel of Taiwan's east coast is
Hualien's Taroko Gorge.（台灣東岸的珍寶是花蓮的
太魯閣峽谷。）【jewel ('dʒuəl) *n.* 瑰寶；珠寶】

3. ***It is a gorge of marble cliffs forming a long valley.***
marble ('mɑrbḷ) *adj.* 大理石的　　cliff (klɪf) *n.* 懸崖；峭壁
form (fɔrm) *v.* 形成　　valley ('vælɪ) *n.* 山谷

　　這句話的意思是「它是一個峽谷，是由大理石懸崖
形成的一個長長的山谷。」也可説成：

Taroko Gorge is a beautiful marble canyon.
（太魯閣峽谷是一個美麗的大理石峽谷。）
It has towering cliffs and a rushing white water
　　river.（它有高聳的懸崖和湍急的白色河流。）
canyon ('kænjən) *n.* 峽谷　　towering ('tauərɪŋ) *adj.* 高聳的
rushing ('rʌʃɪŋ) *adj.* 奔騰的；急速流動的

4. ***The Central Cross Island Highway can lead you to***
   its wonders.

   the Central Cross Island Highway 中部橫貫公路

   lead〔 lid 〕*v.* (路)帶領…(至某地)

   wonder〔'wʌndɚ 〕*n.* 奇觀

   　　這句話的意思是「你沿著中部橫貫公路走，就可以看到
   它的奇景。」也可說成：

   A scenic route to Taroko Gorge is along the
   Central Cross Island Highway.

   (中橫公路是一條前往太魯閣峽谷的風光明媚的道路。)

   Traveling through the mountains on the
   Central Cross Island Highway is a great
   way to get to Taroko Gorge.

   (經由中橫公路穿越群山，是前往太魯閣峽谷最
   棒的一條路。)

   scenic〔'sinɪk 〕*adj.* 風景好的　　route〔 rut 〕*n.* 路；路線
   travel〔'trævḷ 〕*v.* 行進

中部橫貫公路有什麼特別的？

What's special about the Central Cross Island Highway?

This winding mountain road has breathtaking scenery.

It's exciting, spectacular and sometimes scary.

It's one of the most beautiful highways in the world.

**

highway ('haɪ,we) *n.* 公路
winding ('waɪndɪŋ) *adj.* 蜿蜒的
breathtaking ('brεθ,tekɪŋ) *adj.* 令人驚嘆的
scenery ('sinərɪ) *n.* 風景
spectacular (spεk'tækjələ) *adj.* 壯觀的
scary ('skεrɪ) *adj.* 嚇人的

【背景説明】

1. ***What's special about the Central Cross Island Highway?***
   highway (ˈhaɪˌwe) *n.* 公路

   這句話的意思是「中部橫貫公路有什麼特別的？」
   也可説成：

   Why is the Central Cross Island Highway so
   　highly recommended?
   （爲什麼中部橫貫公路得到如此高度的推薦？）

   Is the Central Cross Island Highway a good
   　road to take? (走中部橫貫公路好嗎？)

   highly (ˈhaɪlɪ) *adv.* 高度地；非常
   recommend (ˌrɛkəˈmɛnd) *v.* 推薦　take (tek) *v.* 選取；利用

2. ***This winding mountain road has breathtaking scenery.***
   winding (ˈwaɪndɪŋ) *adj.* 蜿蜒的
   breathtaking (ˈbrɛθˌtekɪŋ) *adj.* 令人驚嘆的
   scenery (ˈsinərɪ) *n.* 風景

   這句話的意思是「這條蜿蜒的山路有令人驚嘆的風
   景。」也可説成：

   It has the most beautiful scenery of any road in
   　Taiwan. (它是台灣風景最美的一條路。)

   This winding road offers gorgeous views.
   （這條蜿蜒的道路呈現了非常美麗的風景。）

   offer (ˈɔfɚ) *v.* 呈現　gorgeous (ˈgɔrdʒəs) *adj.* 非常漂亮的
   view (vju) *n.* 風景

3. *It's exciting, spectacular and sometimes scary.*

exciting〔ɪk'saɪtɪŋ〕*adj.* 令人興奮的;刺激的

spectacular〔spɛk'tækjələ〕*adj.* 壯觀的

scary〔'skɛrɪ〕*adj.* 嚇人的

這句話的意思是「它是令人興奮的、壯觀的,而且有時是可怕的。」也可說成:

Driving this road is really an unforgettable experience.

(在這條路上開車,確實是一個令人難忘的經驗。)

Driving on this incredible and majestic road is never dull.

(在這條驚人且雄偉的路上開車,是絕對不會無聊的。)

unforgettable〔ˌʌnfə'gɛtəbḷ〕*adj.* 難忘的

incredible〔ɪn'krɛdəbḷ〕*adj.* 不可思議的

majestic〔mə'dʒɛstɪk〕*adj.* 雄偉的   dull〔dʌl〕*adj.* 無聊的

4. *It's one of the most beautiful highways in the world.*

這句話的意思是「它是世界上最美的公路之一。」也可說成:

Many claim this road's scenery is the best in the world.

(許多人宣稱,這條路的風景是全世界最棒的。)

【claim〔klem〕*v.* 宣稱】

台灣最有名的山是什麼山？

What's the most famous mountain in Taiwan?

Alishan is Taiwan's top-rated mountain resort.

It has ancient conifer forests and a world famous railway.

The wonderful sunrises, sunsets and "sea of clouds" are out of this world!

**

top-rated ('tɑpˌretɪd) *adj.* 具有最高級別的；受歡迎的
resort (rɪ'zɔrt) *n.* 旅遊勝地　ancient ('enʃənt) *adj.* 古老的
conifer ('kɑnəfɚ) *n.* 針葉樹　railway ('relˌwe) *n.* 鐵路
sunrise ('sʌnˌraɪz) *n.* 日出　sunset ('sʌnˌsɛt) *n.* 日落
sea of clouds 雲海　*out of this world* 極好的

【背景說明】

1. ***What's the most famous mountain in Taiwan?***

   這句話的意思是「台灣最有名的山是什麼山？」也
   可說成：Which mountain area in Taiwan is the
   best to visit? (台灣的哪一個山區是最好的觀光地區？)

2. ***Alishan is Taiwan's top-rated mountain resort.***
   top-rated (ˈtɑpˌretɪd) *adj.* 具有最高級別的；受歡迎的
   resort (rɪˈzɔrt) *n.* 旅遊勝地

   這句話的意思是「阿里山是台灣最好的山區旅
   遊勝地。」也可以說：The Alishan area is
   considered the best. (阿里山區被認為是最好的。)
   【consider (kənˈsɪdɚ) *v.* 認為】

3. ***It has ancient conifer forests and a world famous
   railway.***
   ancient (ˈenʃənt) *adj.* 古老的
   conifer (ˈkonəfɚ) *n.* 針葉樹
   forest (ˈfɔrɪst) *n.* 森林　　railway (ˈrelˌwe) *n.* 鐵路

   這句話的意思是「它有古老的針葉樹森林和世界
   知名的鐵路。」也可說成：

   The mountain forests of Alishan are full of
   magnificent cedar, cypress and pine trees.
   (阿里山的山區森林充滿了壯觀的杉木、柏樹和松樹。)

The forest railway is about 45 miles long
　　and it has about 80 bridges and 50 tunnels.
（這條森林鐵路約長四十五英哩，而且它通過約
　　八十座橋和五十個隧道。）

magnificent〔mæg'nɪfəsṇt〕*adj.* 壯觀的
cedar〔'sidɚ〕*n.* 杉木　　cypress〔'saɪprəs〕*n.* 柏樹
pine〔paɪn〕*n.* 松樹　　mile〔maɪl〕*n.* 英哩（約等於 1.6 公里）
tunnel〔'tʌnḷ〕*n.* 隧道

**4. *The wonderful sunrises, sunsets and "sea of clouds"
are out of this world!***

sunrise〔'sʌn‚raɪz〕*n.* 日出　　sunset〔'sʌn‚sɛt〕*n.* 日落
sea of clouds 雲海　　*out of this world* 極好的

　　這句話的意思是「令人驚嘆的日出、日落和雲海，
真是太棒了。」也可說成：

The beautiful sunrise and sunset at Alishan
　　are very famous in Taiwan.
（阿里山美麗的日出和日落是台灣知名的。）

The famous "sea of clouds" is also an
　　impressive sight you'll never forget.
（著名的「雲海」景觀也是令人印象深刻，
　　你將永生難忘。）

impressive〔ɪm'prɛsɪv〕*adj.* 令人印象深刻的
sight〔saɪt〕*n.* 景象

台灣最有名的湖是什麼湖？

What's the most famous lake in Taiwan?

Sun Moon Lake, at 2,500 feet, is Taiwan's best lake.

It has sparkling green water with a gorgeous mountain backdrop.

The lake is shaped like a sun and a moon.

**

Sun Moon Lake 日月潭
sparkling (ˈspɑrklɪŋ) *adj.* 閃耀的
gorgeous (ˈgɔrdʒəs) *adj.* 非常漂亮的
backdrop (ˈbækˌdrɑp) *n.* 背景   shape (ʃep) *v.* 使成…形

【背景説明】

1. ***What's the most famous lake in Taiwan?***

   famous〔'feməs〕*adj.* 有名的　　lake〔lek〕*n.* 湖

   　　　這句話的意思是「台灣最有名的湖是什麼湖？」
   也可說成：

   Does Taiwan have any nice lakes I can visit?
   （台灣有任何不錯的湖我可以去觀光的嗎？）

   Are there any freshwater lakes in Taiwan?
   （台灣有任何淡水湖嗎？）

   【freshwater〔'frɛʃˏwɔtə〕*adj.* 淡水的】

2. ***Sun Moon Lake, at 2,500 feet, is Taiwan's best lake.***

   　　　這句話的意思是「二千五百英呎高的日月潭是台
   灣最好的湖。」也可說成：

   Sun Moon Lake is nestled high up in the
   mountains.（日月潭高高地坐落在山中。）

   The picturesque lake is a top tourist spot.
   （這個風景如畫的湖是一流的觀光景點。）

   nestle〔'nɛsl̩〕*v.* 坐落於
   picturesque〔ˏpɪktʃə'rɛsk〕*adj.* 如畫的
   top〔tɑp〕*adj.* 最高級的；居首位的
   tourist〔'turɪst〕*adj.* 觀光的

3. *It has sparkling green water with a gorgeous mountain backdrop.*

sparkling (ˈspɑrklɪŋ) *adj.* 閃耀的
gorgeous (ˈgɔrdʒəs) *adj.* 非常漂亮的
backdrop (ˈbæk͵drɑp) *n.* 背景

　　這句話的意思是「它有閃耀的綠色湖水和非常美麗的山當背景。」也可以說：

It's a crystal clear lake with lots of fish.
（它是一個有很多魚，而且如水晶般清澈的湖。）

The surrounding mountains give Sun Moon Lake a perfect "postcard" appearance.
（周圍的山讓日月潭呈現出完美「明信片」的樣貌。）

Sun Moon Lake is a natural lake with magnificent surrounding mountains.
（日月潭是一個被壯麗群山所圍繞的天然湖。）

crystal (ˈkrɪstl̩) *adj.* 水晶似的　　clear (klɪr) *adj.* 清澈的
surrounding (səˈraʊndɪŋ) *adj.* 圍繞的；周圍的
postcard (ˈpost͵kɑrd) *n.* 明信片
magnificent (mægˈnɪfəsn̩t) *adj.* 壯麗的

4. *The lake is shaped like a sun and a moon.*

shape (ʃep) *v.* 使成…形

　　這句話的意思是「這湖的形狀像是一個太陽和一個月亮。」也可說成：Sun Moon Lake gets its name from the lake's shape.（它因為湖的形狀而被取名為日月潭。）

65 台灣有哪些主要的離島？

What are the main islands off Taiwan?

Taiwan has the Penghu islands to the southwest.

There are Green Island and Orchid Island to the southeast.

Kinmen and Matsu are to the west, near mainland China.

**

off〔ɔf〕*prep.* 在…之外　Penghu〔'pʌŋ'hu〕*n.* 澎湖
southwest〔͵sauθ'wɛst〕*n.* 西南方　***Green Island*** 綠島
orchid〔'ɔrkɪd〕*n.* 蘭花　***Orchid Island*** 蘭嶼
southeast〔͵sauθ'ist〕*n.* 東南方　Kinmen〔'kinmən〕*n.* 金門
Matsu〔'mætsu〕*n.* 馬祖　west〔wɛst〕*n.* 西方
mainland〔'men͵lænd〕*n.* 大陸　***mainland China*** 中國大陸

【背景說明】

1. *What are the main islands off Taiwan?*

   main〔men〕*adj.* 主要的　　island〔'aɪlənd〕*n.* 島

   off〔ɔf〕*prep.* 在…之外

   　　這句話的意思是「台灣有哪些主要的離島？」

   也可說成：

   Does Taiwan have any main islands around it?

   （台灣周圍有任何主要的島嶼嗎？）

   Please tell me the major islands surrounding

   　　Taiwan.（請告訴我台灣周圍的主要島嶼。）

   around〔ə'raʊnd〕*prep.* 在…周圍

   surround〔sə'raʊnd〕*v.* 環繞

2. *Taiwan has the Penghu islands to the southwest.*

   Penghu〔'pʌŋ'hu〕*n.* 澎湖　　*to the southwest* 在西南方

   　　這句話的意思是「台灣的西南方有澎湖群島。」

   也可說成：

   Penghu is also called the Pescadores Islands.

   　　（澎湖又叫做澎湖群島。）

   Penghu islands is located halfway between

   　　Taiwan and mainland China.

   　　（澎湖群島位在台灣和中國大陸的中間。）

   Pescadores〔͵pɛska'dɔrɪz〕*n. pl.* 澎湖群島

   be located 位於　　halfway〔'hæf'we〕*adv.* 在中途

   mainland〔'men͵lænd〕*n.* 本土；大陸

3. ***There are Green Island and Orchid Island to the***
   southeast.
   Green Island 綠島   orchid (ˈɔrkɪd) *n.* 蘭花
   Orchid Island 蘭嶼   southeast (ˌsaʊθˈist) *n.* 東南方
   to the southeast 在東南方

   這句話的意思是「東南方有綠島和蘭嶼。」以下
   是相關資訊：

   The waters around Green Island have over 300
   varieties of fish and about 203 species of coral.
   （綠島周圍的海域有超過 300 種的魚和大約 203 種的珊瑚。）

   On Orchid Island you can see the traditional life
   style and culture of the Yami aborigines.
   （在蘭嶼，你可以看見雅美族傳統的生活方式和文化。）

   waters (ˈwɔtəz) *n. pl.* 海水   variety (vəˈraɪətɪ) *n.* 種類
   species (ˈspiʃɪz) *n.* (動植物的) 種   coral (ˈkɔrəl) *n.* 珊瑚
   life style 生活方式   aborigine (ˌæbəˈrɪdʒənɪ) *n.* 原住民

4. ***Kinmen and Matsu are to the west, near mainland***
   China.
   Kinmen (ˈkɪnmən) *n.* 金門   Matsu (ˈmætsu) *n.* 馬祖
   west (wɛst) *n.* 西方   mainland (ˈmenˌlænd) *n.* 大陸

   這句話的意思是「金門和馬祖在西邊，靠近中國大
   陸。」也可說成：Kinmen and Matsu are extremely
   close to mainland China. （金門和馬祖離中國大陸非
   常近。）【extremely (ɪkˈstrimlɪ) *adv.* 非常地】

Question 66　台灣最有名的博物館是哪個？

> What's the most famous museum in Taiwan?

> The National Palace Museum is world-renowned.
>
> It houses over 700,000 ancient Chinese treasures.
>
> It has priceless paintings, calligraphy, jade, bronzes, porcelain, etc.

** ———————————————

palace (ˋpælɪs) *n.* 宮殿　***world-renowned*** 世界知名的
house (haʊz) *v.* 收藏　ancient (ˋenʃənt) *adj.* 古代的
treasure (ˋtrɛʒɚ) *n.* 寶藏　priceless (ˋpraɪslɪs) *adj.* 無價的
calligraphy (kəˋlɪgrəfɪ) *n.* 書法　jade (dʒed) *n.* 玉
bronze (brɑnz) *n.* 銅器　porcelain (ˋpɔrslɪn) *n.* 瓷器

【背景説明】

1. ***What's the most famous museum in Taiwan?***
   famous ('feməs) *adj.* 有名的
   museum (mju'ziəm) *n.* 博物館

   這句話的意思是「台灣最有名的博物館是哪個？」
   也可以説：

   What's the best art or history museum in
     Taiwan? (台灣最好的藝術或歷史博物館是哪個？)
   Which museum is regarded as Taiwan's best?
   (哪一個博物館被認爲是台灣最好的？)
   【regard (rɪ'gɑrd) *v.* 認爲】

2. ***The National Palace Museum is world-renowned.***
   palace ('pælɪs) *n.* 宮殿
   world-renowned ('wɜldrɪ'naund) *adj.* 世界知名的

   這句話的意思是「國立故宮博物院是世界知名的。」
   也可説成：

   It's noted as one of the four best museums
     in the world.
   (它以名列世界四大博物館之一而聞名。)
   The National Palace Museum is the world
     leader in Chinese art.
   (國立故宮博物院是全世界中國藝術的先驅。)
   【noted ('notɪd) *adj.* 著名的　leader ('lidə) *n.* 先驅；領導者】

3. ***It houses over 700,000 ancient Chinese treasures.***
house〔haʊz〕*v.* 收藏　　ancient〔'enʃənt〕*adj.* 古代的
treasure〔'trɛʒɚ〕*n.* 寶藏

　　這句話的意思是「它收藏了超過七十萬件古代的中
國寶物。」也可說成：

> There are over 700,000 pieces of priceless
> art in the Palace Museum.
> （故宮博物館有超過七十萬件的無價藝術品。）

> The Palace Museum has over 700,000 artifacts
> and cultural items on display in rotation.
> （故宮博物院有超過七十萬件的藝術品和文物輪流展出。）

art〔ɑrt〕*n.* 藝術品　　item〔'aɪtəm〕*n.* 物品
display〔dɪ'sple〕*n.* 展示　　rotation〔ro'teʃən〕*n.* 輪流
in rotation 輪流地

4. ***It has priceless paintings, calligraphy, jade, bronzes,***
porcelain, etc.
priceless〔'praɪslɪs〕*adj.* 無價的
calligraphy〔kə'lɪgrəfɪ〕*n.* 書法　　jade〔dʒed〕*n.* 玉
bronze〔brɑnz〕*n.* 銅器　　porcelain〔'porslɪn〕*n.* 瓷器
etc. 等等（= et cetera〔ɛt'sɛtərə〕）

　　這句話的意思是「它有珍貴的畫作、書法、玉、
銅器、瓷器等。」也可說成：The Palace Museum
has every type of artifact you can imagine.（只
要你想像得到的各種藝術品，故宮博物院都有。）

【artifact〔'ɑrtɪˌfækt〕*n.* 藝術品　　imagine〔ɪ'mædʒɪn〕*v.* 想像】

Question 67 台北有哪個不錯的廟宇可以參觀？ ∎

What's a good temple to visit in Taipei?

Lungshan Temple in Wanhua is the best.

It's the oldest and most popular temple in Taipei.

It has elaborate decorations, stone columns and carvings.

**

temple〔ˋtɛmpl̩〕*n.* 廟宇　***Lungshan Temple*** 龍山寺
elaborate〔ɪˋlæbərɪt〕*adj.* 精巧的
decoration〔͵dɛkəˋreʃən〕*n.* 裝飾品
column〔ˋkɑləm〕*n.* 圓柱　carving〔ˋkɑrvɪŋ〕*n.* 雕刻

【背景說明】

1. ***What's a good temple to visit in Taipei?***

   temple ('tɛmpl̩) *n.* 廟宇

       這句話的意思是「台北有哪個不錯的廟宇可以參觀?」也可說成:

   Which temple in Taipei is the best?
   (台北最好的廟是哪一間?)

   Can you recommend the best temple to
       visit in Taipei?
   (你能不能推薦我去參觀台北最好的一間廟?)

   【recommend (ˌrɛkə'mɛnd) *v.* 推薦】

2. ***Lungshan Temple in Wanhua is the best.***

       這句話的意思是「萬華的龍山寺是最好的。」也可說成:

   Everyone considers Lungshan Temple to
       be Taipei's premier temple.
   (大家都認為龍山寺是台北最好的廟。)

   Lungshan Temple, which means "dragon Mountain
       temple" is Taipei's most popular temple.
   (Lungshan Temple 意指『龍山寺』,是台北最受
       歡迎的廟。)

   【premier ('primɪɚ) *adj.* 第一的   dragon ('drægən) *n.* 龍】

3. *It's the oldest and most popular temple in Taipei.*

這句話的意思是「它是台北最古老，也是最受歡
迎的廟宇。」也可說成：

Lungshan Temple, built in 1738, is Taipei's oldest.

（龍山寺建於 1738 年，是台北最古老的廟。）

It's a very active temple with many worshippers
every day.

（它是非常興旺的廟，每天都有很多的祭拜者。）

【active (ˈæktɪv) *adj.* 興隆的　worshipper (ˈwɜʃəpə) *n.* 祭拜者】

4. *It has elaborate decorations, stone columns and carvings.*

elaborate (ɪˈlæbərɪt) *adj.* 精巧的
decoration (ˌdɛkəˈreʃən) *n.* 裝飾品
column (ˈkɑləm) *n.* 圓柱　carving (ˈkɑrvɪŋ) *n.* 雕刻

這句話的意思是「它有精緻的裝飾品、石柱，和雕
刻。」也可說成：

The architecture of Lungshan Temple's roof
and columns is very elaborate.

（龍山寺屋頂和石柱的建築式樣非常精巧。）

Lungshan Temple's decorations are intricate
and detailed.（龍山寺的裝飾是繁複而精細的。）

architecture (ˈɑrkəˌtɛktʃə) *n.* 建築式樣　roof (ruf) *n.* 屋頂
intricate (ˈɪntrəkɪt) *adj.* 複雜的
detailed (dɪˈteld) *adj.* 詳細的

Question 68 我可以去哪裡泡溫泉？

Where can I soak in a hot spring?

You can find hot springs all over Taiwan.

There are hot, cold , mud and saltwater springs in Taiwan.

They can cure diseases and relax you.

**

soak〔sok〕*v.* 浸泡　　spring〔sprɪŋ〕*n.* 泉水
hot spring 溫泉　　mud〔mʌd〕*n.* 泥巴
saltwater〔'sɔlt,wɔtɚ〕*adj.* 海水的；鹽水的
cure〔kjur〕*v.* 治療　　disease〔dɪ'ziz〕*n.* 疾病
relax〔rɪ'læks〕*v.* 使放鬆

【背景説明】

1. ***Where can I soak in a hot spring?***

   soak〔sok〕*v.* 浸泡　spring〔sprɪŋ〕*n.* 泉水

   這句話的意思是「我可以去哪裡泡溫泉？」也可
   以説：Where can I take a nice hot spring bath?
   （我可以去哪裡洗個舒服的溫泉澡？）
   Where can I find a nice hot spring?
   （哪裡可以找到不錯的溫泉？）

2. ***You can find hot springs all over Taiwan.***

   這句話的意思是「你可以在全台灣各地發現溫
   泉。」也可説成：

   There are natural hot springs in many areas
   of Taiwan.（在台灣的許多地區有天然溫泉。）

   There are nice hot springs in many locations
   around Taiwan.（在台灣的很多地方有不錯的溫泉。）

   The top hot springs are at Wu Lai, Chipen,
   Yangming Mountain, Peitou, Chiaohsi, etc.

   （排名前幾名的溫泉在烏來、知本、陽明山、北投、礁溪等等。）

   location〔lo'keʃən〕*n.* 地點　around〔ə'raund〕*prep.* 在…四處

3. ***There are hot, cold, mud and saltwater springs in Taiwan.***

   mud〔mʌd〕*n.* 泥巴　saltwater〔'sɔlt,wɔtɚ〕*adj.* 海水的

   這句話的意思是「台灣有溫泉、冷泉、濁泉和海水溫
   泉。」也可説成：

Taiwan has many types of springs, including hot, cold, mud and saltwater springs.
（台灣有許多種泉，包括溫泉、冷泉、濁泉和海水溫泉。）

Taiwan has a cold spring in Suao, a mud spring in Guanziling and a saltwater spring on Green Island.
（台灣在蘇澳有冷泉，在關仔嶺有濁泉，在綠島則有海水溫泉。）

4. ***They can cure diseases and relax you.***
cure〔 kjʊr 〕v. 治療　　disease〔 dɪˈziz 〕n. 疾病
relax〔 rɪˈlæks 〕v. 使放鬆

這句話的意思是「他們可以治療疾病並使你放鬆。」
也可說成：

Natural springs are very therapeutic.
（天然泉是非常有療效的。）

The minerals in the springs can help treat skin diseases, arthritis, neuralgia and rheumatic aches.
（泉水中的礦物質有助於治療皮膚病、關節炎、神經痛，和風濕痛。）

therapeutic〔 ˌθɛrəˈpjutɪk 〕adj. 有療效的
mineral〔ˈmɪnərəl 〕n. 礦物質　　arthritis〔 arˈθraɪtɪs 〕n. 關節炎
neuralgia〔 njʊˈrældʒə 〕n. 神經痛
rheumatic〔 ruˈmætɪk 〕adj. 風濕（性）的

69 台灣有哪些類型的大眾運輸工具？

> **What forms of public transportation does Taiwan have?**

> There are major highway, rail and air services.
>
> Each city has a convenient bus system.
>
> Taipei's MRT system is world-class.

**

form〔fɔrm〕*n.* 形式
transportation〔ˌtræspɚˈteʃən〕*n.* 運輸工具
highway〔ˈhaɪˌwe〕*n.* 公路　　rail〔rel〕*n.* 鐵路
air〔ɛr〕*n.* 空中　　service〔ˈsɝvɪs〕*n.* 公共事業
MRT 捷運（ = *Mass Rapid Transit*）
world-class〔ˈwɝldˌklæs〕*adj.* 世界級的；具有世界水準的

【背景説明】

1. ***What forms of public transportation does Taiwan have?***
form〔 fɔrm 〕 *n.* 形式；種類
transportation〔͵træspəˋteʃən 〕 *n.* 運輸工具

這句話的意思是「台灣有哪些類型的大衆運輸工具？」也可説成：

Does Taiwan have good transportation systems?
（台灣有不錯的運輸系統嗎？）

Is public transportation in Taiwan pretty good?
（台灣的大衆運輸非常好嗎？）
【pretty〔ˋprɪtɪ 〕 *adv.* 相當；非常】

2. ***There are major highway, rail and air services.***
highway〔ˋhaɪ͵we 〕 *n.* 公路　　rail〔 rel 〕 *n.* 鐵路
air〔 ɛr 〕 *n.* 空中　　service〔ˋsɝvɪs 〕 *n.* 公共事業；航班；行駛

這句話的意思是「有主要的公路、鐵路和航空運輸。」也可説成：

Taiwan has modern, well-built highway
and railway systems.
（台灣有既現代而且建造精良的公路及鐵路系統。）

You can go almost anywhere in Taiwan by
road, train or airplane.（你幾乎可以經由陸路、
火車或飛機到台灣的每一個地方。）
well-built〔ˋwɛlˋbɪlt 〕 *adj.* 建造精良的
railway〔ˋrel͵we 〕 *n.* 鐵路

3. *Each city has a convenient bus system.*

這句話的意思是「每一座城市都有便利的公車系
統。」也可說成：

Public buses are inexpensive and go almost
everywhere.
（公共汽車不貴，而且幾乎可以到任何地方。）
Every major city, town and village is accessible
　by some bus route.
（每一個主要的城市、鄉鎮和村莊經由某些公車路線，
　都很容易到達。）

inexpensive (ˌɪnɪk'spɛnsɪv) *adj.* 不貴的；便宜的
accessible (æk'sɛsəbl) *adj.* 容易到達的　route (rut) *n.* 路線

　　cheap 和 inexpensive 都是表示「便宜的」，但是前
者具有「不值錢的」意味，而後者純粹是表示「不貴的」。

4. *Taipei's MRT system is world-class.*

這句話的意思是「台北的捷運系統是世界級的。」
也可說成：

The Mass Rapid Transit system in Taipei is
　excellent. (台北的大眾捷運是極好的。)
The MRT system is clean, efficient and
　comfortable.
（大眾捷運系統是乾淨、有效率，而且舒適的。）

mass (mæs) *adj.* 大眾的　rapid ('ræpɪd) *adj.* 快速的
transit ('trænsɪt) *n.* 運輸　efficient (ə'fɪʃənt) *adj.* 有效率的

Question 70 離開台灣要帶什麼紀念品比較好？

What's a good souvenir to leave
Taiwan with?

Try calligraphy scrolls, watercolor
paintings or pottery.

Also, name chops or aboriginal
handcrafts are nice.

Finally, buy a bag of Oolong tea or
some peanut candy.

**

souvenir (ˌsuvəˈnɪr) *n.* 紀念品
calligraphy (kəˈlɪgrəfɪ) *n.* 書法   scroll (skrol) *n.* 卷軸
watercolor (ˈwatɚˌkʌlɚ) *adj.* 水彩的   pottery (ˈpatɚɪ) *n.* 陶器
chop (tʃap) *n.* 印章   aboriginal (ˌæbəˈrɪdʒən!) *adj.* 原住民的
handcraft (ˈhændˌkræft) *n.* 手工藝品

【背景説明】

1. ***What's a good souvenir to leave Taiwan with?***

   souvenir〔ˌsuvəˈnɪr〕*n.* 紀念品；特產

   　　這句話的意思是「離開台灣要帶什麼紀念品比較
   好？」也可說成：

   What are some nice things to buy in Taiwan?
   （台灣有哪些不錯的東西可以買？）

   What are popular things for tourists to
   　　purchase in Taiwan?
   （在台灣，有哪些東西是觀光客普遍會購買的？）

   【purchase〔ˈpɝtʃəs〕*v.* 購買】

2. ***Try calligraphy scrolls, watercolor paintings or pottery.***

   calligraphy〔kəˈlɪgrəfɪ〕*n.* 書法　　scroll〔skrol〕*n.* 卷軸
   watercolor〔ˈwɑtɚˌkʌlɚ〕*adj.* 水彩的
   pottery〔ˈpɑtɚɪ〕*n.* 陶器

   　　這句話的意思是「試看看書法卷軸、水彩畫，或陶
   器。」也可說成：

   Chinese art always makes an excellent souvenir.
   （中國藝術品總是能成爲最棒的紀念品。）

   Try buying some pottery plates, bowls or vases
   　　made at Yingee.
   （試著買些鶯歌製的陶盤、陶碗，或陶製的花瓶。）

   【plate〔plet〕*n.* 盤子　bowl〔bol〕*n.* 碗　vase〔ves〕*n.* 花瓶】

3. *Also, **name chops or aboriginal handcrafts are nice**.*

also〔'ɔlso〕*adv.* 並且；另外　　chop〔tʃɑp〕*n.* 印章
name chop 姓名印章
aboriginal〔ˌæbə'rɪdʒənḷ〕*adj.* 原住民的
handcraft〔'hænd͵kræft〕*n.* 手工藝品

　　這句話的意思是「而且，印章或是原住民的手工藝品也不錯。」也可說成：

> A Chinese name chop is a fun and special
> memento.
> （中國的姓名印章是有趣而且特別的紀念品。）
> Craftwork by the aborigines is considered a
> great souvenir.
> （原住民的手工藝品被認為是很棒的紀念品。）

fun〔fʌn〕*adj.* 有趣的　　memento〔mɪ'mɛnto〕*n.* 紀念品
craftwork〔'kræftwɜk〕*n.* 手工藝品
aborigine〔æbə'rɪdʒəni〕*n.* 原住民

4. *Finally, **buy a bag of Oolong tea or some peanut candy**.*

　　這句話的意思是「最後，買一包烏龍茶或一些花生糖。」也可以說：

> Most Taiwanese love Oolong tea and consider
> it a nice gift.
> （大部分台灣人喜歡烏龍茶，而且認為它是不錯的禮物。）
> Peanut candy is a tasty souvenir to buy.
> （花生糖可以買來做為美味的紀念品。）

【tasty〔'testɪ〕*adj.* 美味的；好吃的】

台灣小吃中英對照表

碗　粿	Bowl Steamed Flour Cake
肉　粽	Glutinous Rice Dumpling
油　飯	Glutinous Oil Rice
冬　粉	Green Bean Noodles
粄　條	Flat Noodles
炒米粉	Fried Rice Noodles
餛飩麵	Wonton Noodles

*　　　*　　　*

刀削麵	Sliced Noodles
海產粥	Seafood Congee/ Seafood Rice Soup
魯肉飯	Braised Pork Rice
陽春麵	Plain Noodles
排骨麵	Noodles with Pork Rib
牛肉麵	Beef Noodles

*　　　*　　　*

麻醬麵	Sesame Paste Noodles
蚵仔麵線	Oyster Thin Noodles
豬腳麵線	Pork Knuckle Noodle Threads
蛋炒飯	Egg(s) Fried Rice
四神湯	Four Herbs Soup
藥燉排骨	Stew Ribs with Herbs

花枝羹　Squid Thick Soup / Squid Potage
肉　圓　Round Dumpling with Meat
酸辣湯　Sour and Spicy Soup
魚丸湯　Fish Ball Soup
紫菜蛋花湯　Seaweed & Egg Soup
排骨酥湯　Crispy Sparerib Soup
當歸鴨　Angelica Duck

　　　　*　　　*　　　*

鹽水雞　Boiled Salted(Salty) Chicken
鹽酥雞　Fried Salted(Salty) Chicken
麻油雞　Stew Chicken with Sesame Oil
蘿蔔糕　Fried White Radish Patty
豬血糕　Pigs Blood Cake
筒仔米糕　Rice Tube Pudding
棺材板　Coffin Cake
割　包　Chinese Burger

　　　　*　　　*　　　*

滷　味　Soya-mixed
春　捲　Spring Roll
飯　糰　Rice Ball / Rice and Vegetable Roll
蚵仔煎　Oyster Omelet
臭豆腐　Stinky Tofu
麻辣豆腐　Spicy Hot Tofu
水　餃　Boiled (Chinese) Dumplings

茶葉蛋	Tea Egg
皮　蛋	100-year Egg
鹹鴨蛋	Salted Duck Egg
豆　干	Dried Tofu
燒　餅	Clay Oven Cakes
油　條	Fried Crullers
饅　頭	Steamed Buns

*　　*　　*

肉　鬆	Dried Shredded Pork
愛　玉	Vegetarian Gelatin
糖葫蘆	Calabash Sticks
湯　圓	Rice-Flour Dumpling Soup
豆　花	Tofu Pudding
豆　漿	Soybean Milk
米　漿	Rice & Peanut Milk
冬瓜茶	White Gourd Tea

*　　*　　*

青草茶	Herbal Tea
甘蔗汁	Sugar Cane Juice
楊桃汁	Star Fruit Juice
酸梅汁	Dried Plum Tea
木瓜牛奶	Papaya Milk
珍珠奶茶	Pearl Milk Tea
剉　冰	Shaved Ice

||||||||||||||● 學習出版公司門市部 ●||||||||||||||||

台北地區：台北市許昌街 10 號 2 樓　TEL：(02)2331-4060・2331-9209

台中地區：台中市綠川東街 32 號 8 樓 23 室
　　　　　TEL：(04)2223-2838

|||||||||||||||||||||||||||||||||||||||||||||||||||||||||||

講英文、說台灣

主　　　編／蔡惠婷

發　行　所／學習出版有限公司　　　　☎ (02) 2704-5525

郵 撥 帳 號／0512727-2 學習出版社帳戶

登　記　證／局版台業 2179 號

印　刷　所／裕強彩色印刷有限公司

台 北 門 市／台北市許昌街 10 號 2F　　☎ (02) 2331-4060・2331-9209

台 中 門 市／台中市綠川東街 32 號 8F 23 室　　☎ (04) 2223-2838

台灣總經銷／紅螞蟻圖書有限公司　　☎ (02) 2795-3656

美國總經銷／Evergreen Book Store　☎ (818) 2813622

本公司網址　www.learnbook.com.tw

電 子 郵 件　learnbook@learnbook.com.tw

售價：新台幣二百八十元正

2004 年 12 月 1 日初版

ISBN 957-519-806-9